S0-BYQ-116

PACEMAKER® PRACTICAL ARITHMETIC SERIES

Buying with Sense

Carol L. King

GLOBE FEARON

Globe Fearon Educational Publisher
A Division of Simon & Schuster
Upper Saddle River, New Jersey

PACEMAKER® PRACTICAL ARITHMETIC SERIES

Money Makes Sense

Using Dollars and Sense

Working Makes Sense

Buying with Sense

Director of Editorial and Marketing, Special Education: Diane Galen
Marketing Manager: Susan McLaughlin
Assistant Marketing Manager: Donna Frasco
Executive Editor: Joan Carrafiello
Senior Editor: Stephanie Petron Cahill
Contributing Editor: Jennifer McCarthy
Editorial Assistant: Brian Hawkes
Production Director: Kurt Scherwatzky
Production Editor: John Roberts
Art Supervision: Pat Smythe
Cover Design: A Good Thing Inc.
Interior Design: Thompson Steele Production Services
Electronic Page Production: Thompson Steele Production Services
Illustrators: Thompson Steele Production Services, Karl Nicholason,
   Sam Masami Daijogo, and Diana Thewlis

Printed in the United States of America

 3 4 5 6 7 8 9 10   00 99 98

ISBN 0-8359-3472-1

CONTENTS

All the people in the world have at least one thing in common. All people are consumers. The rich and the poor are consumers. Both students and teachers are consumers. Even babies are consumers.

Consumers are people who use up goods and services. The food you eat is the best example of **consumer goods.** You buy the food and use it up to meet your needs.

If you hire a painter to paint your house, you are using a **consumer service.** You are using up the painter's time and work.

Consumers are in the news a lot during periods of inflation. **Inflation** means that prices are going up, up, up. Consumers never seem to have enough money. How can people pay such high prices for the things they need—things like food, clothes, cars, and houses? Today, everyone needs consumer education.

Consumer education tells you how to get more goods and services for your money. It also tells you how to get *better* goods and services: food that will keep you healthy, clothes that will last a long time, cars that use less gas.

And how do you know you are getting more for your money? You use **consumer math** to find out. In the food store, math tells you whether the 2-pound can really costs less than two 1-pound cans. When you paint your house, math tells you whether it costs less to buy your own paint or to let the painter buy it.

Consumer math deals with dollars and cents, which are written in *decimal* numbers. You'll find some examples on the next page. But if you need help with decimals, be sure to let your teacher know.

Sometimes using consumer math means adding large numbers or figuring percentages. Using a calculator can save time and help you make sure your answers are correct. It is always a good idea to use a calculator to check your work.

Are you ready, fellow consumers? If so, turn the page, and let's start *Buying with Sense.*

- You can add a decimal point *to the right* of any whole number (25 = 25.).
- You can add zeros *to the right* of any decimal point (25. = 25.0 or 25.00 or 25.000).
- The word *digit* means any single number (0, 1, 2, 3, 4, 5, 6, 7, 8, or 9).

Addition: Line up the decimal points then add the columns.

```
    23.1          $4367.09
     5.126          135.55
  2691.333           22.86
+   67.50      +      3.98
  2787.059        $4529.48
```

Subtraction: Line up the decimal points then subtract columns.

Example: $456.78 − $63.29
```
$456.78
− 63.29
$393.49
```

Example: $25 − $13.95
```
$25.00  (add zeros)
− 13.95
$11.05
```

Multiplication: Line up the numbers. Do not worry about lining up the decimal points. Multiply the two numbers.

Count the total digits to the right of both decimal points. Place the decimal point in the answer so that there are as many digits to the right of the decimal point as the total in both numbers that you multiplied.

```
$234.56    (2 digits to the right)
×    4.1    (1 digit to the right)
 23456
 93824
$961.696   (3 digits to the right)
```

Division: To divide by a whole number, add a decimal point and as many zeros as you need to the number being divided. Place the decimal point in your answer directly over the decimal point in the number being divided.

```
       13.636  = 13.64 (rounded off)
11)150.000
   11
   40
   33
    70
    66
    40
    33
     7     STOP HERE*
```

To divide by a decimal number, move the decimal point in every figure the same number of places until you are dividing by a whole number.

```
        13.043  = 13.04 (rounded off)
11.5.)150.0.000
     115
     350
     345
      500
      460
      400
      345
       55    STOP HERE*
```

*A RULE FOR THIS BOOK

Go to three decimal places. Then round off your answer.

- Look at the third digit after the decimal point.
- If the third digit is 5 or more, add .01 to your answer (13.636 = 13.64).
- If the third digit is 4 or less, drop it (13.043 = 13.04).

CHAPTER 1

The Cost of Living

Preview: Average Incomes

The "average American" earned $20,817 in 1994. Here is a list of average incomes for the 50 states and the District of Columbia. Answer these questions about the list.

Per Capita Personal Income by States	
State	**1994**
Alabama	$18,010
Alaska	23,788
Arizona	19,001
Arkansas	16,986
California	22,492
Colorado	22,333
Connecticut	29,402
Delaware	22,828
D.C.	31,136
Florida	21,677
Georgia	20,251
Hawaii	24,057
Idaho	18,231
Illinois	23,784
Indiana	20,378
Iowa	20,265
Kansas	20,896
Kentucky	17,807
Louisiana	17,651
Maine	19,663
Maryland	24,933
Massachusetts	25,616
Michigan	22,333
Minnesota	22,453
Mississippi	15,838
Missouri	20,717
Montana	17,865
Nebraska	20,488
Nevada	24,023
New Hampshire	23,434
New Jersey	28,038
New Mexico	17,106
New York	25,999
North Carolina	19,699
North Dakota	18,546
Ohio	20,928
Oklahoma	17,744
Oregon	20,419
Pennsylvania	22,324
Rhode Island	22,251
South Carolina	17,695
South Dakota	19,577
Tennessee	19,482
Texas	19,857
Utah	17,043
Vermont	20,224
Virginia	22,594
Washington	22,610
West Virginia	17,208
Wisconsin	21,019
Wyoming	20,436

1. What was the average income in your state in 1994? _____

2. Was your state above or below average? _____

3. How many states (including the District of Columbia) were above average in income? _____

4. How many states were below average in income? _____

5. Which state had the highest average income? _____

6. Which state had the lowest average income? _____

7. What was the average income in Oregon? _____

8. What was the average income in these three states?

Nevada _____

Iowa _____

Alabama _____

ANSWERS:

1. answers vary 2. answers vary 3. 24 4. 27 5. D.C. 6. Mississippi 7. $20,419 8. Nevada, $24,023; Iowa, $20,265; Alabama, $18,010

The Cost of Living

Bill Rossi came home from the army early in April. It was great to be home again! Bill was ready for a good, long rest. But late in May his father asked him, "When are you going to get a job?"

Bill laughed. "Don't worry! I'll get a job one of these days."

Bill had saved some money in the army. But by the end of June, he had spent his savings.

So Bill took a **part-time job** driving a delivery truck for $6.00 an hour. The $120 he earned each week was enough for spending money. "And it keeps my father off my back," said Bill.

Then in November, everyone noticed a sudden change in Bill. He was still driving the delivery truck part time. But he had begun to read the "help-wanted" ads every day. Some mornings he got dressed up in his best clothes and went out to look for work. He often made trips to the **state employment office.** It seemed as if Bill had only one thing on his mind—getting a **full-time job.** But that wasn't quite true.

| Words to Know | About Cost of Living |

part-time job: a job that is usually less than eight hours a day and sometimes less than five days a week.

state employment office: an office run by the state to help people find jobs.

full-time job: usually a job that lasts eight hours a day, five days a week—or a total of 40 hours a week.

work-study program: a plan offered by either a company or a school that lets a person work half a day and study half a day.

income: the amount of money a person earns.

estimate: a number that is just a guess. An estimate helps you make plans. For example, before you go on a trip, you make an estimate about how much money you will need to take along.

studio: a very small apartment. Sometimes a studio is just one room plus a tiny kitchen and a bathroom. A studio is sometimes called an efficiency apartment.

townhouse: an apartment that is like a house, but close to other apartments. Often a townhouse is a two-story apartment.

unfurnished apartment: an apartment that is rented without furniture.

furnished apartment: an apartment that is rented with furniture already in it.

afford: to be able to pay the cost.

average: the middle point is found by dividing the sum of a set of figures by the number of figures in the set. For example, 5 is the average of 1, 2, 3, 4, 5, 6, 7, 8, and 9.

1	2	3	4	5	6	7	8	9

Bill was also thinking about getting married. He was in love with a young woman named Jennifer.

"I can't get married on $120 a week," said Bill. "But how much money does a married couple need?" He asked some friends, but each one gave him a different answer.

Jennifer was in school on a **work-study program.** She went to classes in the morning. Then in the afternoon, she worked in a TV and VCR store. She worked 20 hours a week and earned $5.25 an hour. To finish her course, she would have to stay in school until June 15. After that, she would get a better job.

But right now it was Bill who had to find a better job. And not just any job—one that paid enough so that he and Jennifer could get married and live on their own.

But how much is "enough"?

Finally Bill asked his mother. "How much money does a married couple need to live on their own?" His mother gave him this "rule of thumb":

"Figure out how much it will cost you to rent an apartment. That's about how much you need to earn each week. The average family pays at least one week's **income** per month for rent. Of course, it's just an **estimate**—a guess. But an estimate helps you to make plans for the future."

Bill and Jennifer used newspaper ads to find out how much apartments cost. At first the ads were not much help. There were too many ads and too many prices. They could rent a furnished **studio** for $390 a month. Or a "luxury **townhouse**" with one bedroom, **unfurnished,** for $1,500 a month.

"A studio is fine for one person," said Jennifer. "But it's probably too small for the two of us."

"We don't need a luxury townhouse," said Bill. "And besides—we don't have any furniture."

Next they looked at ads for one-bedroom **furnished** apartments. There were not so many of those. They didn't want the worst apartment in town. And they knew they couldn't **afford** the best. How much would it cost to rent an apartment that was just **average?** They decided to figure out the average rent for furnished one-bedroom apartments.

First they made a list of the rents of the ten apartments in the ads. They added up the list of ten prices. Then they divided by 10 to get the average rent. The answer was $497.50. Since it was just an estimate, they rounded it off at $500. Together, Bill and Jennifer would need to earn about $500 a week.

Apartments—Furnished

ALMADEN area—3 room apt. $415. Mature-thinking employed. No pets. 555-3261.

CIVIC Center 1 bdrm. $515, no pets, 1525 N. 1st. 555-2677.

DOWNTOWN 742 S. 9th. 1 br. Furn/unfurn. Very clean. $575 Lease. 555-3615.

FIRST & Willow. 1 br., air-cond., $490. 555-2715.

JULIAN/N. 26th   555-8584
1 & 2 br. from $520, no pets.

NEAR UNIVERSITY, Lrg. 1 br., upstrs. nicely furn. $390. 555-7012.

SUPERB LOCATION
EXTRA SPACIOUS ROOMS, THICK CARPETS, AIR COND. WALLPAPER, 2-DOOR REFRIGERATORS, PRIVATE PATIOS, LUSH LANDSCAPING, FURNITURE AVAILABLE
2 BDRM. FROM $715
1 BDRM. FROM $560

THE APARTMENT
450 NO. MAIN AVE.
555-3030

WESTSIDE. 1 BR. in quiet 6-plex. No pets. $500. 555-8780.

WESTSIDE spac. Jr. 1 br. W&G pd., A-C, no pets. $440. 555-6034.

GLEN AREA
Clean   Quiet
1 & 2 br. furn. only w/garden court. Conven. loc. to 280 and 17. Pool; air, dishw. or patio. Starting $570. 555-6991.

$ 415
515
575

490
520
390

560

500
440

570
+
$4,975

```
              497.50  average rent
        10)4975.00
             40
             ___
             97
             90
             ___
             75
             70
             ___
             50
             50
             ___
              0
```

The **cost of living** is not the same all over the United States. In some cities, the cost of living is very high. In some small towns, it is lower.

Of course, rent is only one of many costs. But you can use rents to **estimate** the cost of living in your area.

Here are ten ads for furnished one-bedroom apartments in a California city. To find the average rent:

a. List all the rents and add them up.

b. Divide your answer by the number of apartments listed. There are ten.

Apartments—Furnished	Rents
ALMADEN Exp. 1 br., quiet, util. paid. $715. 555-0926	_____
FOUNTAIN PARK, 1, 2, Br. from $565. 555-1000. 1026 Franklin St.	_____
DOWNTOWN $540. Cln. 1 bdrm. W/G pd. 470 N. 34th St., aft. 5	_____
DOWNTOWN 1 bdrm. Parking. Refers. $600. 555-3100 Agent	_____
DOWNTOWN—No. 4th St. 1 bdrm., partly furn. $415/mo. 555-0577 or 555-1797 aft. 5 p.m.	_____
SO. 15th St. 1 Bdrm. Clean. $535. 555-1327	_____
STATE UNIVERSITY: 3½ rms. No pets. $515 on lease. Apply 421 East Orchard St.	_____
VALLEY MEDICAL Center. 1 br. clean. No pets. $470. Aft. 4 p.m. 555-5592	_____
WESTSIDE, lrg. studio, AEK, incl. DW. ww cpts. incl. Kit/ba. pool & port. No pets. Quiet living. $640. 555-1438	_____
WESTSIDE, spac. Jr. 1 br. W&G pd., A/C. No pets. $490. 555-6034	_____

Total _____

1. The average rent is _____ .

Cost-of-Living Words

cost of living: the average cost of food, rent, and other needs paid by a person or family.

weekly rent: rent paid each week.

base pay: the amount of a paycheck before taxes are taken out. Base pay is sometimes called *gross* pay.

federal income tax: a tax each worker pays to the federal government. The tax is called a *withholding tax* because it is taken out of (withheld from) your paycheck.

social security tax: a tax that helps old people and others who are in need. The tax is taken out of each paycheck. The tax law is called FICA (Federal Insurance Contributions Act).

disability tax: a tax that helps people who get sick or hurt and must stop working for a time.

take-home pay: the amount of a paycheck after taxes are taken out. Take-home pay is the amount of money that a worker can "take home" and spend. It is also called *net* pay.

Here are ads from two cities in Ohio—one is a large city and the other is a small city.

In these ads, some of the apartments are rented by the week. There are 4.3 weeks in a month. To estimate the cost per month, multiply the **weekly rent** by 4.3.

Is the cost of living higher in the small city or in the big city? Let's find out. Find the average rent for each city.

Example:

$$\begin{array}{r} \$70 \quad \text{a week} \\ \times\ 4.3 \quad \text{weeks in a month} \\ \hline 210 \\ 280 \\ \hline \$301.00 \end{array}$$

(add decimal point and a zero)

Small City

Rent per Month

Apartments—Furnished

All utilities paid, 3 rooms. $85 weekly plus deposit. No pets. 555-5395.

All utilities paid, 2 and 3 rooms, private bath. $70 wk. plus dep. No pets. 555-5395, 555-5665.

Bellville: Nice clean 2 Room Unit, Carpet, utilities paid. $420. Call 555-4241 or 555-7171.

Brand new 1 bdrm., all appliances. 300 Wood St. $400. All utilities paid except electric. 555-0208.

SOUTHSIDE Upper single 3 Room Apt. Private Ent. Utilities Paid. $362.50 plus Dep. 555-5325.

UPPER 2 or 3 bedroom, on South Adams near Park Ave. East, $70 per week, or $280 per mo., plus gas and elec. $125 dep. Metropolitan assistance possible, 555-0845.

1 BEDROOM efficiency, $490 mo. plus deposit. Utilities paid. West location. Call 555-4687.

1 bedroom furnished apartments. Carpeted, utilities paid, $80 a week. Call 555-2544.

2 and 3 room apts. W 3rd, single only. All utilities paid. No pets. $65 weekly plus $50 deposit. Phone 555-0677 or 555-5560.

3 ROOMS and bath, gas and elec. paid, $540, Wayne St. area. Deposit required. 555-0566.

Total _____

Big City

Rent per Month

Rent Furnished Apts.

1 BEDROOM, furnished, $415 mo. plus deposit. Utilities paid. 183 Rowland Ave. 555-4687.

Furnished suites with carpeting, utilities, from $520. Open 9 to 5 daily. Call 555-7700.

APT.

Completely furnished 2 and 3 rooms, free utilities, near bus. From $79 week. Whittier Ave.

CALL 555-8657

APTS. NICE Efficiency, 2-3 rms. $115 per week
FREE ELECTRIC AND GAS
Rec. rm. with pool table. Friendly, homey place to live. Good neighborhood. Ample parking, nice furnishings. 24-hr. security. Embassy, 4311 Prospect.   555-1430

DOWNTOWN—FREE UTILITIES 2-3 rm. Quiet, decorated, laundry, $530. 555-0054.

DULUTH, 7111; $440 month, all utilities. 555-8866.

EUCLID, 13441. Efficiencies. No pets. Bus, rapid. $360 plus security. 555-4424.

EUCLID, 3844 Belmont: 555-4550. Convenient 2- and 3-rm. apts. Includes utilities, linens. $95 wk.

105 E. Cedar, 3 rms., utilities paid. $80 wk. 555-8557.

SHAKER Blvd. Executive efficiency, utilities. $515. 555-0114.

Total _____

2. The average rent in the small city is

_____ .

3. The average rent in the big city is

_____ .

4. Is the cost of living higher in the small city or in the big city?

_____ .

Remember that an estimate is just a guess. Many people spend more than one week's income per month on rent. Others spend less.

Let's look at Apartment A and Apartment B in a building called Villa Rosa. The apartments are just alike. Both apartments rent for $500 a month.

5. Ms. Smith lives in Apartment A. She earns $1,928 a month. How much does she earn in one week? _____

$$4.\ 3\overline{)1928}$$

6. Mr. and Mrs. Jones live in Apartment B. Together, they earn $2,172 each month. How much do they earn in one week? _____

7. Who spends more than one week's income on rent? _____

Jennifer and Bill know what they want. Together, they want to take home at least $500 a week. For now, Jennifer will keep her part-time job. Bill will look for full-time work.

8. Jennifer earns $5.25 an hour. She works 20 hours each week. How much does she earn each week? _____

$$\begin{array}{r} \$5.25 \\ \times\ 20 \\ \hline \end{array}$$

Jennifer gets a paycheck every two weeks. Her **base pay** is $210. But three kinds of taxes are taken out of her check:

federal income tax	$28.50
social security tax	8.93
disability tax	+ 2.28

9. How much money is taken out of each paycheck? _____

10. How much is Jennifer's take-home pay for two weeks? (Subtract total taxes from $210.) _____

11. How much is Jennifer's **take-home pay** for one week? (Divide her take-home pay by 2.) _____

12. If Jennifer and Bill need $500 a week, how much will Bill have to earn each week in take-home pay? (Subtract Jennifer's take-home pay from $500.) _____

debt: amount of money that a person owes to others.

charge account: a plan that lets you pay by using credit cards instead of paying cash.

manage money: how a person handles money by spending and saving.

life insurance: a plan that pays money to a family if one member of the family dies.

health insurance: a plan that pays for doctors and hospital care if a person is sick or gets hurt.

Jennifer was trying to read a book on the bus. It was hard to keep her mind on her homework. She could hear two angry voices. A young man and a young woman were sitting in the seats behind her. Their voices were soft—but very angry.

"Now we'll *never* get out of debt!" the young woman said. "How *could* you spend all that money on a tape deck? We need every cent we've got just to pay our bills!"

"Well, it's not my fault we've got bills!" the young man said. "It's *you* and those charge accounts! At least I paid cash for the tape deck!"

"But we don't *need* a tape deck!" the woman answered. "I used the charge accounts to buy things we really needed!"

The two angry voices went on and on. Later, Jennifer told Bill about the fight she had heard on the bus. Then she said, "It's not easy for young people to manage money. As kids, we didn't get any practice in running a home and paying the bills."

"It looks like we've got a lot to learn," Bill answered. "So we'd better start learning right now!"

The next day Jennifer stopped at the school library. She told the librarian, "I'm going to get married soon. Bill and I want to learn how to run a home and manage money."

The librarian gave Jennifer a small book that explained how most families spend their income.

This table shows that families have different needs. A big family with a small income might spend 30% of their money on food. A small family with a big income might spend only 15% on food.

How a Family Spends Its Money*	
Expense	**Percent of Income**
Housing	15–40%
Utilities	4–7%
Food	15–30%
Transportation	6–10%
Household and personal needs	2–4%
Health care	5–15%
Clothing	3–9%
Savings	5–9%
Recreation	4–7%
Big items for the home	2–8%

*Many families have other costs: life insurance, health insurance, gifts, church and charities, education, union dues, and others.

Bill and Jennifer would like to earn at least $500 a week in take-home pay. That would be about $26,000 a year (based on 52 weeks in a year). They can use $2,150 as an estimate of their **monthly income.** (This is based on 4.3 weeks in a month times $500 per week.) Then they can use **percentages** of $2,150 to estimate their **expenses.**

You may use a calculator to figure large sums or to check your work.

Example: If they spend 25% of their income on rent, how much rent will they pay?

$$\begin{array}{r} \$2150 \\ \times\ .25 \\ \hline 10750 \\ 43000 \\ \hline \$537.50 \end{array}$$

1. Utilities

Utilities are gas, electricity, water, telephone, and garbage and recycling pickup.

Find the cost of utilities at 4% of $2,150 ($2,150 × .04). _____

2. Food

Food covers meals eaten in restaurants as well as meals eaten at home.

Estimate the cost of food at 19% of $2,150. _____

Money Words

monthly income: the amount of money a person earns in a month.

percentages: parts of a whole written in hundredths. For example, one half shown as a percentage is 50%.

expenses: costs that must be met in order to live.

budget: a plan for spending and saving.

3. Transportation

Transportation covers everything you pay to drive a car—if you have one. You pay for the car, insurance, license, repairs, gas and oil, and parking. Jennifer and Bill do not have a car. For $25 a month, a person can buy a pass to ride on the city buses. Jennifer and Bill buy bus passes. Sometimes they borrow a car and buy gas for it.

Find the cost of transportation at 3% of $2,150. _____

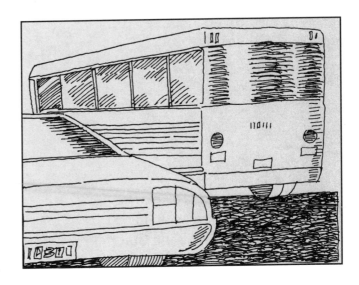

4. Household and Personal Needs

Laundry and dry cleaning are examples of household needs. "Personal needs" means haircuts and most drugstore items except medicine.

Estimate these expenses at 3.5% of $2,150 ($2,150 × .035). _____

5. Health Care

"Health care" pays the doctor and the dentist. This item also pays for health insurance, hospital bills, and medicine.

Estimate health care at 6% of $2,150. _____

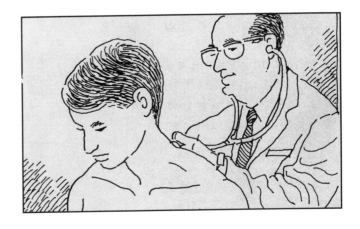

6. Clothing

This item covers clothes and shoes. It also covers shoe repair and goods for sewing.

Estimate clothing costs at 7% of $2,150. _____

7. Savings

Savings is money set aside for hard times or for problems that might come up.

Estimate savings at 12% of $2,150. _____

8. Recreation

Jennifer and Bill like to watch cable TV, go to sporting events, movies, concerts, and dancing. They want to take vacation trips. Crafts and hobbies also come under "recreation."

Estimate recreation costs at 5% of $2,150. _____

9. Big Items for the Home

Jennifer and Bill will want to buy many things after they start a home of their own. For example, they would like to buy a color TV set.

Estimate "big items for the home" at 4.5% of $2,150. _____

10. You have just made a **budget** for Jennifer and Bill. A budget is a plan for spending and saving. Now add all ten items to see how much money you have set aside in your budget.

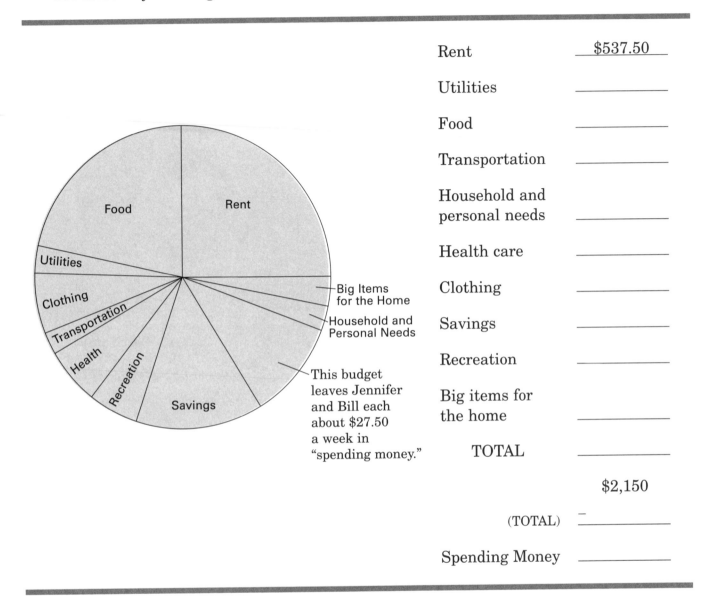

Rent	$537.50
Utilities	_____
Food	_____
Transportation	_____
Household and personal needs	_____
Health care	_____
Clothing	_____
Savings	_____
Recreation	_____
Big items for the home	_____
TOTAL	_____
	$2,150
(TOTAL)	_____
Spending Money	_____

Subtract your total from $2,150. Did you get $236.50? Then that amount is *not* part of the budget—at least, not yet. The $236.50 would give Jennifer and Bill each $118.25 a month for "pocket money." That's about $27.50 a week for each person ($118.25 ÷ 4.3).

Each person in a family should have some spending money that is not part of the budget. Jennifer would need some of her "pocket money" for school. Sometimes Bill or Jennifer will want to buy gifts. They may want to give money to a church or another good cause.

Suppose your income was $2,150 a month. Would this sample budget work for you? Probably not.

The budget in this chapter was made from estimates, and an estimate is just a guess. To make a *real* budget, you need facts and figures.

Start *today* to keep track of the money you spend. Buy a little notebook. Keep it in your pocket or purse. Write down the amounts you spend. Ask your family if they are willing to carry notebooks and keep track of their spending.

In Chapter 5, you will find some charts to write your figures on. For more help with budgeting, read the charts now. You can use these charts when you make your own budget.

Consumer Tip

Both Bill and Jennifer plan to work. They hope to work for companies that give health insurance and life insurance to their employees. If not, Jennifer and Bill will buy their own insurance.

Health insurance can help lower the cost of health care expenses. Jennifer and Bill should not wait too long to buy life insurance. It costs very little when you are young but more as you get older.

Food

Date

½ — 16.50

⅙ — 32.18

⅐ — 4.87

Household and Personal Needs

Date

½ Shampoo 1.69

1/9 Detergent 3.49

Everyone needs recreation, and everyone likes to have fun. But it's easy to see your recreation dollars slip away like magic.

For example, here's a story about Jim and Sally Jinx. Jim and Sally both work, but they have trouble keeping up with their bills. This is what they did last weekend.

Jim and Sally were planning to go camping on their vacation. They had saved $125 to buy a tent. On Saturday morning they went to the sporting goods store and bought a tent on sale for $74.99.

In the store they saw tennis rackets and balls on sale. "I've never played tennis," Sally said. "But I think I'd like to try it."

"Me, too," said Jim. "We didn't spend all our savings on the tent. Let's buy tennis rackets and balls." They bought two tennis rackets and one can of three balls.

On Saturday night they went to a concert. They "saved money" by buying the cheapest seats—two tickets for $16.50 each.

On Sunday afternoon Jim and Sally played tennis. They went to the city courts. There they didn't have to pay for a court. It was a very hot day, and they had to wait a long time for a court to play on. Later, they decided they didn't like tennis very much.

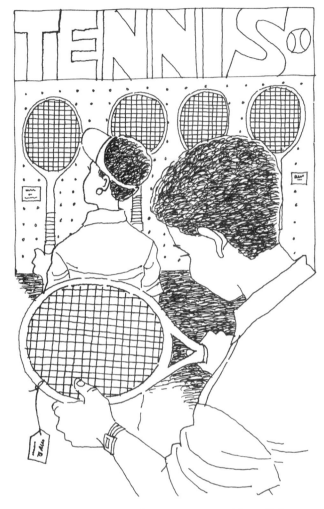

> **Consumer Tip**
> Recreation costs add up very quickly. Watch this part of your budget closely. It can help to figure out the cost of your recreation before you spend the money.

"We've spent a lot on recreation this weekend," Jim said. "Tonight, let's just stay home."

"OK," Sally said. "We'll have a cold drink and listen to music."

Jim stopped at a store to buy a six-pack of soda. While he was there, he bought bottled water for Sally, too.

While Jim was buying the drinks, Sally saw a music store that was open. Tapes and CDs were on sale. Sally thought it would be fun to have some new music to listen to. She bought four tapes to surprise Jim.

Later, Jim added up what they had spent on the weekend. He said, "I guess we won't be able to pay the phone bill this month."

Use the prices in the ads to answer these questions:

1. How much did Jim and Sally spend at the sporting goods store? _____

2. How much did they spend on two tickets for the concert? _____

3. How much did they spend on cold drinks and tapes for a quiet evening at home? _____

4. How much did they spend for *all* of these things? _____

TWO PERSON 5' x 7' NYLON TENT

"A" frame front with Rain Fly. Zippered screen front door, complete with pole, stake & tent bag.

REG. $89.99
SALE
$74.99

TENNIS RACKETS

Quality graphite frame with leather grips. Nylon strung.

$49.99
YOUR CHOICE
REG. $69.99

$2.19
TENNIS BALLS
CAN OF 3
Reg. $2.99, LIMIT 4 CANS

CDs
$11.89

CASSETTE TAPES
$7.99 EA.

MOUNTAIN WATER **$1.09**

SPRING WATER

SALE PRICED

COLA 6-PACK

12 OZ. CANS
SALE PRICED
$1.89

THE DON CLARK SHOW
AUGUST 11–13
Fri. 8:30, Sat. 7 & 10:30
$16.50 & $22.50

Would two people need to spend $150.50 a month on clothes? That's 75.25 for each person.

Bill thought that number sounded high. He said, "I don't spend very much on clothes. Most months, I don't buy any clothes at all."

"How often do you buy clothes?" Jennifer asked.

"Maybe four times a year," Bill answered. "Spring, summer, winter, and fall."

Bill shops for clothes once every three months. With this budget, he could spend $225.75 on each shopping trip. (But Bill probably buys clothes more often than he thinks he does.)

Sometimes Bill takes shoes to the repair shop to get them fixed. Shoe repair is part of the clothing budget.

In fact, shoes are a big part of your clothing budget. If you are short of cash, you can wear last year's clothes a while longer. But shoes wear out. You have to buy new ones.

Consumer Tip
Buy the best shoes you can afford. You get only one pair of feet to last you all your life.

$58.95

$54.90

$47.99

$45.50

$39.99

EXERCISE 4

1. Suppose Bill bought these five pairs of shoes in one year. How much would he spend on shoes?

2. Now divide your answer by 12. How much of this monthly clothes budget would he spend on shoes?

REDUCED UP TO 75% OFF

A   B   C   D

Winter clothes like these go on sale in the spring. People buy them and put them away until the following winter.

3. Suppose Jennifer had bought these clothes last year. Which items would still be in style today? Check the items you feel are still in style.

_____ A   _____ C

_____ B   _____ D

4. Here are the regular prices of these clothes. How much would all nine items cost at regular prices?

A. Vest	$39	
Jacket	$48	
Pants	$41	
B. Jacket	$50	
Shirt	$32	
Skirt	$35	
C. Shirt	$20	
Skirt	$55	
D. Coat	$152	
TOTAL	_____	

5. How much would all nine items cost at 20% off? (Multiply $472 by .20 to get 20%. Then subtract that amount from $472.) _____

6. How much would all nine items cost at 30% off? _____

7. How much would all nine items cost at 75% off? _____

Once, long ago, drugstores sold only medicine. Today, big drugstores sell everything but the kitchen sink!

The budget in this book divides regular drugstore items into two groups:

1. Items that you use as medicine. These items belong under "health care" in the budget.

2. Items that you use to keep your body clean or make it look better. These items belong under "personal needs" in the budget.

Consumer Tip

If you watch TV, you hear the names of many drugstore items. But you pay extra for any item that is sold on TV. TV time costs a lot of money. This cost is passed along to you and other shoppers.

These items are "personal needs." You could save money by buying them at the sale prices in these ads.

1. If you bought one of each item, how much would you spend? _____

Here are some more "personal needs" at
sale prices.

SHAMPOO OR CONDITIONER

20 OZ. BOTTLE $2.39

FACE LOTION

4 OZ. BOTTLE $3.99

SUNTAN LOTION
SPF 15 OR SPF 30

4 OZ. $2.99

TOOTHBRUSH ADULT SIZE

SALE PRICE $1.67

HAIRSPRAY
ASSORTED FORMULAS

9 OZ. CAN
SALE PRICE $1.29

LIPSTICKS
CREAMS AND FROSTS

YOUR CHOICE $2.99

SAFETY SWABS
DOUBLE TIPPED COTTON

SALE PRICE $1.95
PKG. of 300

LOTION NEW IMPROVED!

SALE PRICE $2.89
4 OZ. SIZE

2. If you bought one of each
item, how much would
you spend? _____

Do you buy items like these from the drugstore?
If so, add them to the cost of health care.

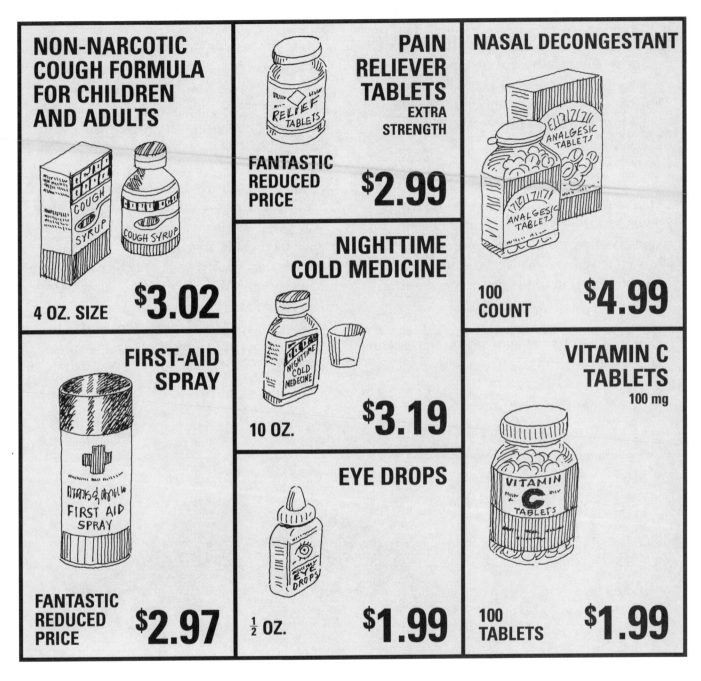

NON-NARCOTIC COUGH FORMULA FOR CHILDREN AND ADULTS

4 OZ. SIZE $3.02

FIRST-AID SPRAY

FANTASTIC REDUCED PRICE $2.97

PAIN RELIEVER TABLETS EXTRA STRENGTH

FANTASTIC REDUCED PRICE $2.99

NIGHTTIME COLD MEDICINE

10 OZ. $3.19

EYE DROPS

½ OZ. $1.99

NASAL DECONGESTANT

100 COUNT $4.99

VITAMIN C TABLETS 100 mg

100 TABLETS $1.99

3. If you bought one of each item in this ad, how much would you spend? _____

1. Bill could rent an apartment for $400 a month or less. Why did he use the *average* cost of furnished one-bedroom apartments to estimate his future needs? Which is better—a high estimate or a low estimate?

2. Clip stories about the cost of living from your newspaper. Are prices going up or down? Is the change in prices fast or slow? Which item in the family budget has changed the most in the last year? How do families change their spending as the cost of living changes?

3. Suppose you have spent all the money in your clothing budget. Then you see the winter coats on sale for half-price. You know you will need a new coat next winter. Would you buy a winter coat now? Is there any way you could buy the coat now and still stay within your budget?

4. Does your family have a cat or a dog? If so, find out how much it costs you to keep a pet. How much do you spend on pet food each month? Do you spend money on health care for your pet? If so, how much? Where do these costs belong in your family budget? Would you list them under *health care* and *food*? Or would you list them under *recreation?* Explain your answer.

TEST YOURSELF

Practice making a sample budget.
Let's suppose you earn $1,540 a month in take-home pay.
Use these percentages to find out how much you would spend
on every item listed.

1. Rent, 21% _____

2. Utilities, 5% _____

3. Food, 19% _____

4. Transportation, 15% _____

5. Household and personal needs, 3% _____

6. Health care, 8% _____

7. Clothing, 9% _____

8. Savings, 6% _____

9. Recreation, 4% _____

10. Big items for the home, 7% _____

11. Now add up all ten items.
    How much money have you
    set aside in this budget? _____

12. How much money is left for
    spending money? _____

ANSWERS:

1. $323.40 2. $77 3. $292.60 4. $231 5. $46.20
6. $123.20 7. $138.60 8. $92.40 9. $61.60
10. $107.80 11. $1,493.80 12. $46.20

Put an X beside the correct answer.

1. What is an estimate?

_____ **a.** a guess

_____ **b.** a rule that people should always follow

_____ **c.** an average

_____ **d.** a percentage

2. Where does a movie ticket belong in the family budget?

_____ **a.** under "transportation"

_____ **b.** under "savings"

_____ **c.** under "recreation"

_____ **d.** under "personal needs"

3. What is take-home pay?

_____ **a.** the same as base pay

_____ **b.** the amount of the paycheck after taxes are taken out

_____ **c.** the hourly rate

_____ **d.** the average pay before taxes are taken out

4. What is a budget?

_____ **a.** a percentage of take-home pay

_____ **b.** a plan that lets you shop with credit cards instead of paying cash

_____ **c.** amounts of money that a person owes to others

_____ **d.** a plan for spending and saving

5. How much would food cost for a big family with a small income?

_____ **a.** about 2% of base pay

_____ **b.** a high percentage of take-home pay

_____ **c.** a low percentage of take-home pay

_____ **d.** 98% of base pay

6. Where does soap belong in the family budget?

_____ **a.** under "utilities"

_____ **b.** under "health care"

_____ **c.** under "food"

_____ **d.** under "personal needs"

ANSWERS:

1.a 2.c 3.b 4.d 5.b 6.d

CHAPTER 2

Finding a Job

Preview: Help Wanted

Answer these questions by writing "yes" or "no" on each blank.

RESTAURANT short-order cook and relief waitress/waiter position. Part-time, breakfast & lunch. 555-3485 after 12 noon.

1. John goes to school from 8:00 A.M to 3:00 P.M. Could he work at this restaurant?

_____

RESTAURANT—Sandwich Shop (NO WEEKENDS) Part-time sandwich makers, Monday thru Friday, 11 a.m.-2 p.m. Possible full-time position. 555-3345 before 11 a.m. or after 1 p.m.

2. Jan needs a full-time job right away. Should she try to get this job?

_____

RETAIL CLERK, experienced, full-time, all shifts. Apply in person, 1195 N. Richland St. M/F, EOE

3. Jeff wants to work nights. Should he try to get this job?

_____

SALES CLERK, Retail Sports Store, Ski, Tennis, & Backpacking experience necessary. Full or part-time. 555-7300.

4. Jean does not ski or play tennis. Could she work at this store?

_____

SALES CLERK, retail store & cash register exp. FT, no Sun. or evenings. Gen'l duties. 555-4872.

5. Jack has never had a job before. Should he try to work at this store?

_____

SALES CLERK exp. refs. Apply in person. Plaza Pharmacy, 1902 S. College Ave. 555-2772.

6. Joan wants to work in a drugstore. Should she apply for this job by writing a letter to Plaza Pharmacy?

_____

SALES CLERK, full/part-time. Apply Bartons' Books, 7892 E. Fig Street, 555-2039, between 10 and 4.

7. Jerry wants to go job hunting during his lunch hour. Could he apply for this job?

_____

ANSWERS:

1. no 2. no 3. yes 4. no 5. no 6. no 7. yes

Finding a Job

Bill had very little **work experience.** After high school he joined the army. Now he wasn't sure what kind of work he wanted to do. He wanted a "good job"—but what kind of jobs are really good? After talking it over with Jennifer, Bill made a plan. In his job hunt, he would look for work that:

- was fun to do,
- paid enough to live on,
- gave him a chance to learn new skills,
- would lead to a better job in the future.

Bill studied the help-wanted ads. He was looking for the word *trainee.* A trainee is someone who gets paid while learning a new job. Often the trainee ads say:

"Will train."
"Learn a trade."
"No experience needed."

There were three kinds of trainee jobs with good pay: selling, training for **management,** and learning a trade. Bill soon learned that a lot of other people wanted jobs in management and sales. Often the jobs were given to college graduates, or to people with experience. Next, Bill thought he would try learning a trade.

One day the Hiram **Employment Agency** ran two good ads in the paper. Bill took a bus downtown to Hiram's office. There he talked to Jerry. Jerry asked him

LUMBER/WOOD TECH. TRAINEE
Learn a trade/no layoffs/$815.
Call Jerry. 555-8300. Fee. Hiram
Agency—350 Winslow St.

MACHINIST TRAINEE TO $953
4-day week. Paul. 555-8300. Fee.
Hiram Agency—350 Winslow St.

Words to Know	When Finding a Job

work experience: what a person has learned from a past job.

management: the people who run a business. These workers plan what the business should try to do and how to do it best.

employment agency: a group of people who help others find jobs. Private employment agencies charge fees for their service. Public (or state) employment agencies do not charge fees.

contract: a paper that two people sign to show what they have agreed to do. By law, both people must obey the terms of the contract.

employer: a person or company who hires people for a job.

fee: a charge for services.

employee: a person who works for a company or another person.

---

to fill out some forms. When Bill had done that, Jerry said, "Here's your **contract.** Sign on this line." Bill signed the paper, and Jerry gave him a copy of it. Bill read it as he rode home on the bus.

What a surprise! Bill found out what would happen if Jerry got him a job. Bill would have to pay the agency more than a whole month's pay!

Employment agencies earn their money two ways: Sometimes the **employer** pays the **fee.** Sometimes the **employee** pays it. Bill had learned two lessons:

- Look for help-wanted ads that say "fee paid" or "no fee."
- Never sign a contract without reading it.

The Hiram Employment Agency ran this ad in the paper. Watch out for that word *fee!* For this job, Hiram's fee is 140% of the monthly pay. If you earn $835 a month, their fee is $1,169.

> ASSEMBLY TRAINEE/$835
> Good eyesight & steady hands.
> No experience needed. Fee.
> Hiram Agency—350 Winslow St.

$$\begin{array}{r} \$835 \\ \times\ 1.40 \\ \hline 33400 \\ 835 \\ \hline \$1,169.00 \end{array}$$

Here are Hiram's fees, based on monthly pay.

Monthly Pay		Percentage of Monthly Pay
0 to	749.99	100%
750 to	999.99	140%
1,000 to	1,249.99	180%
1,250 to	1,499.99	220%
1,500 to	1,749.99	260%
1,750 to	1,999.99	280%
2,000 and up		300%

Study Hiram's fees based on monthly pay. Find the fee for each of these jobs:

1. Bank teller
   trainee / $894 _____

$$\begin{array}{r} \$894 \\ \times\ 1.40 \\ \hline \end{array}$$

2. Credit authorizer
   trainee / $1,075 _____

$$\begin{array}{r} \$1,075 \\ \times\ 1.80 \\ \hline \end{array}$$

3. Restaurant management
   trainee / $2,000 _____

$$\begin{array}{r} \$2,000 \\ \times\ 3.00 \\ \hline \end{array}$$

4. Word processor / $1,500 _____

$$\begin{array}{r} \$1,500 \\ \times\ 2.60 \\ \hline \end{array}$$

Here are Hiram's fees, based on yearly pay.

Yearly Pay	Percentage of Yearly Pay
0 to 8,999.99	8.33%
9,000 to 11,999.99	11.66%
12,000 to 14,999.99	15.00%
15,000 to 17,999.99	18.33%
18,000 to 20,999.99	21.66%
21,000 to 23,999.99	23.33%
24,000 and up	24.00%

Study Hiram's fees, based on yearly pay. Find the fee for each of these jobs. You may use a calculator.

5. Payroll trainee / $16,800 _____

$16,800
× .1833

6. Head custodian / $13,549 _____

$13,549
× .15

7. Sales/auto parts / $18,200 _____

$18,200
× .2166

8. Production manager /
$36,400 _____

$36,400
× .24

Bill hoped he would not have to pay a large fee to an employment agency. He decided to ask his friends how they had found their jobs. Afterwards he made a list of all the different places to find out about job openings.

Where to Learn About Job Openings

- Parents, friends, and neighbors
- School placement services
- Help-wanted ads
- Employment agencies
- State employment service offices
- Civil service announcements (federal, state, local)
- Labor unions
- Professional associations (state and local chapters)
- Libraries and community centers
- Counseling and employment programs
- Youth programs
- Employers

Page 32

Jennifer wanted to finish high school. But she also wanted to marry Bill. She began to think about dropping out of school. She talked to Mrs. Gast, the **vocational counselor** at school.

"I can type 35 words per minute," Jennifer said. "Could I get a full-time job in an office?"

"You might get a job doing general office work," Mrs. Gast said. "But you will have a better chance at getting a job and a higher salary if you have a diploma. To do well in an office today, you should learn to use a **computer.** Many office jobs involve data processing on a computer."

At work Jennifer asked Alan Rowe, the TV repairer, how he learned to fix TV sets.

> ### Words to Know — About Job Skills
>
> **computer:** a machine that stores and processes facts.
>
> **vocational counselor:** someone who helps you decide which job is right for you.

"I went to a technical school," Alan said. "I worked during the day and took classes at night. I studied electronics."

Later Jennifer told Bill, "Alan went to night school. Now he earns $12.85 an hour. And I only get $5.25!"

"You just gave me a good idea," Bill said. "Maybe I'll take some night classes."

"I'm going to finish high school," Jennifer said. "And after high school, I'm going to study electronics."

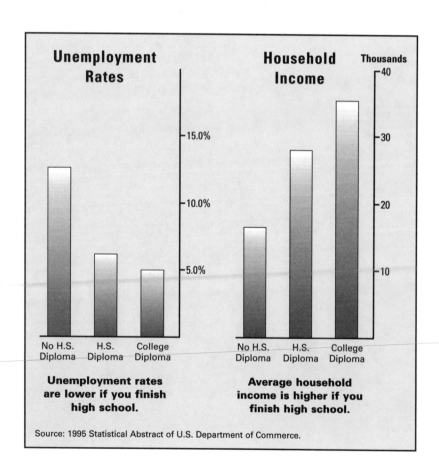

Unemployment Rates

15.0%
10.0%
5.0%

No H.S. Diploma
H.S. Diploma
College Diploma

Unemployment rates are lower if you finish high school.

Household Income

Thousands
40
30
20
10

No H.S. Diploma
H.S. Diploma
College Diploma

Average household income is higher if you finish high school.

Source: 1995 Statistical Abstract of U.S. Department of Commerce.

Consumer Tip

Ask your school **vocational counselor** which skills are needed in your city. See the *Occupational Outlook Handbook* in your library. It will tell you which jobs should be easy to find.

1. Here are four jobs for clerks. The monthly starting pay is given for each job.

Clerk/type 45 wpm (words per minute)	$1,292
Clerk/word processing	$1,502
Clerk/accounting	$1,416
Clerk/data entry	$1,386

What is the average monthly pay for these jobs? _____

2. Here are four jobs for administrative assistants. The starting pay is given for each job.

Administrative Assistant/ must type 60 wpm	$1,585
Administrative Assistant/ office management	$1,781
Administrative Assistant/ spreadsheet background	$1,931
Administrative Assistant/ word processing	$2,079

What is the average monthly pay? _____

People who fix TV sets are paid by the hour. There are 173.3 working hours in one month. For example, Alan Rowe earns $12.85 an hour. Working full time, he earns $2,226.91 a month.

$12.85   an hour
× 173.3   hours per month
3855
3855
8995
1285
$2,226.905 = $2,226.91 (rounded off)

3. Use the hourly pay in the chart below. Find out how much each job pays by the month. Then write the amount in the blanks on the chart.

Job	Hourly Pay	Monthly Pay
Line Cook	$6.75	_____
Security Guard	$7.00	_____
Hotel Clerk	$6.50	_____
Auto Mechanic	$15.00	_____
Dental Lab Technician	$11.00	_____
Computer Operator	$14.50	_____

Bill drove the delivery truck on Monday, Wednesday, and Friday. On Tuesday and Thursday he looked for a full-time job. He never seemed to have enough time for job hunting. That was bad enough. But sometimes his boss asked him to work on a Tuesday or Thursday.

One Monday Bill answered, "No, I can't come to work tomorrow." He had made an **appointment** for a job **interview** the next day.

His boss, Mrs. Wells, looked a little angry. She said, "Bill, this is the third time you've turned me down."

"I'm sorry," Bill said. "I have an appointment tomorrow. And it's important." He didn't want to tell Mrs. Wells he was going to quit as soon as he found a better job.

"You're a good worker, Bill," Mrs. Wells said. "But I need someone I can count on when the work is heavy."

Bill thought he was going to get fired. Now he had to tell the truth. "I am planning to get married," he said. "And I can't get married until I find a full-time job. I've been job hunting on Tuesday and Thursday."

Words to Know | **About Job Hunting**

appointment: a meeting planned ahead of time. Two or more people agree to meet at a certain time and place.

interview: a meeting where one person asks questions and another person answers.

benefits: anything a company pays for in order to help the worker. Benefits include paid vacations and holidays, life insurance, health insurance, retirement plans. A company car is one of the benefits that many salespeople get.

retirement plan: an insurance plan that helps to support an older person who no longer works.

foreman: a worker who tells other workers what to do and how to do it. Sometimes a foreman is called a *supervisor.*

"So that's what you're up to!" Mrs. Wells began to smile. "Would you like to work for me full time?" Bill couldn't believe his ears.

If he worked full time, he'd make $240 a week. Would that be enough? "Can you pay me $7 an hour?" he asked.

"Not now," Mrs. Wells shook her head. "But you will get a raise in six months. Beginning July 1, I'll pay you $7 an hour. And if you work full time, you'll get **benefits**—you know, paid vacations and holidays, life insurance, and health insurance. We even have a **retirement plan.** The benefits are worth quite a lot."

Bill remembered the plan he had made. He asked, "Would this job lead to a better job in the future?"

Mrs. Wells nodded. "I've noticed that you get along well with other workers," she said. "Maybe you would make a good **foreman** some day."

"Then I'll take the job," said Bill.

self-employed: a person who owns a business.

workers' compensation: a plan that covers on-the-job injuries for employees.

Bill gets paid every other Friday. His base pay is $480 (240 × 2 weeks). Four kinds of taxes are taken out of each paycheck: federal income tax, state income tax, social security tax, and disability tax. To find Bill's take-home pay:

a. Add the taxes that Bill pays out of each check.

federal income tax	$70.00
state income tax	$ 4.80
social security tax	$35.00
disability tax	$ 5.76
TOTAL	

b. Subtract the taxes from his base pay ($480).

1. How much money is taken out of Bill's paycheck in taxes? _____

2. How much is Bill's take-home pay? _____

3. How much is his take-home pay for one week? _____

4. Jennifer's take-home pay is $85.15 a week. How much take-home pay do Bill and Jennifer earn together each week? _____

John Wong is **self-employed.** John and his helpers cut grass and do gardening. John earns about $21,000 a year. But he never gets any paid holidays or vacations. And he has to pay for his own insurance and for **workers' compensation.**

The chart below shows how John pays for his insurance.

Insurance	Payment Plan	Cost per Year
Life insurance	$169.35 every 6 months	_____
Health insurance	$95.76 every month	_____
Workers' compensation	$175.00 every month	_____
Retirement plan	$125.00 every month	_____
	TOTAL	_____

5. Using the facts above, how much does John Wong pay for insurance every year? Fill in the blanks on the chart.

1. All kinds of skills are worth money. Some jobs call for everyday skills, such as cooking, child care, washing windows, or driving a car. Make a list of your own skills. What are they? Then read the help-wanted ads in your newspaper. Are there employers in your area who need your skills? If so, cut out these ads.

2. Would you like to learn some new skills? If so, look for trainee ads in your newspaper. Look for ads that say "will train," or "learn a trade," or "no experience needed." More important, look for the kinds of work you think you would like to do. Cut out these ads, too.

3. Part-time jobs often turn into full-time jobs. Have you ever had a part-time job? Did your boss like your work? If you went back to that company, would your boss give you another job? Suppose the company has no openings now. Would you feel free to ask the boss, "May I use your name for a reference?" (A reference is someone who helps you get a job. That person tells others you are a good worker.)

4. Don't give up. Talk to friends and neighbors. Contact public and private employment agencies, or your local library. Look in the Yellow Pages and other directories to find possible employers. Many employers will file your application for future job openings.

Consumer Tip

"Pay" means two things: (1) the money in your paycheck, and (2) benefits, such as retirement plans, paid holidays, and insurance. Of the money the company pays you, about 71% is your paycheck. The other 29% is paid in benefits.

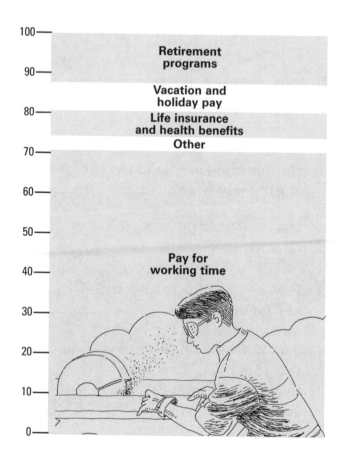

TEST YOURSELF

Work these problems. Then check your answers at the bottom of the page.

1. Terry earns $6.75 an hour. How much does Terry earn in a 40-hour week? _____

2. The Hiram Employment Agency listed these jobs for people who program computers.

Junior/Accounting	$34,000
Financial	$35,000
Mac/IBM	$35,000
Manufacturing	$40,000
Communications	$45,000
Systems Analyst	$50,000
Employers Pay Our Fee	

   What is the average starting pay? _____

3. The Hiram Employment Agency found Frank a job that pays $14,040 a year. Hiram's fee is 11.66% of the yearly starting pay. How much does Frank have to pay the agency? _____

4. A nurse's aide named Gerry earns $6.30 an hour. Gerry works 40 hours each week and gets paid once every two weeks. What is Gerry's base pay? _____

5. Chris, a carpenter, earns $960.00 a week. Chris works 40 hours each week. What is Chris's hourly rate? _____

6. Here are three jobs for truck drivers. Which job pays the most? Write the letter in the blank. _____
   a. Deliveries/$400 wk. (There are 4.3 weeks in a month.)
   b. Deliveries/Warehouse trainee/$6 hr. (There are 173.3 working hours in a month.)
   c. Driver/Sales trainee/$1,039 mo.

ANSWERS:

1. $270 2. $39,833 3. $1,637.06 4. $504 5. $24 6. a

Answer the questions about these ads:

ASSEMBLERS
No experience necessary. Immediate openings for assembler trainees. Day shift. Small mfg. plant. $5.25/hr. Apply 9-11 a.m. Mon.-Fri. 675 Main St.

1. How much experience do you need for this job?

_____

2. When could you start working?

_____

3. How much would you earn in a 40-hour week?

_____

COUNTER—DRY CLEANING
Exper. Able to check and assemble garments. Minor sewing. $5.75 per hr./40 hr. week. Call 555-3254.

4. Could you get this job if you had never worked before?

_____

5. What skill do you need for this job?

_____

6. How much would you earn each week?

_____

CASHIER RECEPTIONIST/Fee
WILL TRAIN/To $950
Norse Agency. 555-9285.

7. Who pays the agency's fee for this job?

_____

8. Do you need experience for this job?

_____

9. Could you get more than $950 a month in starting pay?

_____

CUSTOMER SERVICE
to $980
Clerical, heavy phones. Electronics firm pays our fee. Benefits, raises, profit sharing. Call Pam Morse Agency. 555-9285.

10. Who pays the agency's fee for this job?

_____

11. Might you get less than $980 in starting pay?

_____

12. At $980 a month, how much would you earn in a year?

_____

ANSWERS:

1. None 2. Now 3. $210 4. No 5. Sewing 6. $230 7. Employee 8. No 9. No 10. Employer 11. Yes 12. $11,760

CHAPTER 3

Checking and Savings Accounts

Preview: Writing Checks

Write out these checks from the facts given.

Eva Fayes wrote a check to the Baron Flying School on February 9, 1997. The amount was $67.50.

George Raven wrote a check to Entropy Power Company on April 11, 1997. The amount was $29.27.

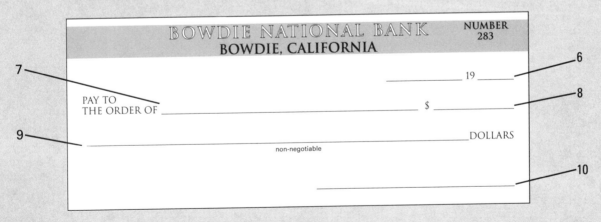

ANSWERS:

1. February 9, 1997   2. Baron Flying School   3. $67.50
4. Sixty-seven and 50/100   5. Eva Fayes   6. April 11, 1997
7. Entropy Power Company   8. $29.27   9. Twenty-nine and 27/100   10. George Raven

Checking and Savings Accounts

On payday, Jennifer and Bill went out to dinner with their friends Jose and Nina. After dinner, Bill took out his billfold to pay for the food. Nina saw that Bill was carrying quite a lot of money.

"Bill, why do you carry so much money?" Nina asked.

"Because today is payday," Bill said.

"But you shouldn't carry so much cash," Nina said. "Suppose you lost your billfold! Suppose somebody robbed you!"

"I guess you're right," Bill said. "I'll open a **bank account** one of these days."

"Nina works in a bank," Jose said. "She knows all about banking."

"Now is a good time to open a **checking account**," said Nina. "Central Bank is ten years old this month. If you open an account this month, you won't have to pay any **service charges.** You might save as much as $60 a year."

"I've been thinking about opening a **savings account**," Jennifer said. "I've been saving money in a piggy bank. But if I put my money in Central Bank, it will earn **interest.**"

"That's true," Nina said. "But your savings would earn only $2\frac{1}{4}\%$ interest at Central Bank. You can get $2\frac{1}{2}\%$ interest from a **savings and loan association.**"

"Good!" said Jennifer. "Bill and I will need the money when we get married."

"When are you two going to get married?" asked Jose.

"Right away," Bill answered.

"Not until I get out of school," said Jennifer. Jose and Nina laughed.

"Well," said Bill, "we're going to get married one of these days."

Banking Words

deposit: the act of putting money in a bank account or the money that you put in a bank account.

statement: a paper that shows bank deposits, checks paid out, and balances. The bank sends a statement to each person who has a checking account.

balance: the amount of money in a bank account.

minimum balance: the lowest amount of money in your bank account at any one time.

When you have a checking account, your bank handles your money for you. It keeps your money safe. The bank pays a bill for you each time you write a check. The bank even does arithmetic for you. It adds all the money you **deposit.** Then it subtracts all the money you spend by writing checks. Each month that bank sends you a **statement** showing how much money is in your account.

For these services, the bank charges a fee called a service charge. The bank explains its service charges when you open your checking account. Usually there is more than one way to pay service charges. You can pick out the plan that is best for you. Let's look at three different plans.

Plan A—$5.00 a month

Your charge is $5.00 each month, no matter how many checks you write or how much money you have in your account.

1. Under Plan A, how much would you pay in service charges for one year? _____

Plan B—$.30 per check

You pay $.30 for every check you write.

2. Under Plan B, how much would you pay:

   a. If you wrote 26 checks in January? _____

   b. If you wrote 12 checks in February? _____

   c. If you wrote 32 checks in March? _____

Plan C—Your service charge depends on the number of checks you write and the **balance** in your account. (Your *balance* is the amount of money in your account at any one time.)

Under Plan C, there is no service charge if you keep a **minimum balance** in your account. Each bank sets its own minimum. You can shop around to find the bank with the lowest minimum balance. The chart on the next page shows minimum balances and service charges for four banks in the same city.

Plan C Service Charges

	Alpha Bank	Beta Bank	Gamma Bank	Delta Bank
Minimum Balance	$500 No charge	$750 No charge	$1,000 No charge	$2,000 No charge
	Under $500	Under $750	Under $1,000	Under $2,000
Monthly charge	$2.50	$6.00	$4.00	$5.00
Charge per check	$ .50	none	$ .30	$ .15

Example: Suppose you have an account at Alpha Bank. In April your minimum balance was $399 and you wrote 20 checks. You would pay a monthly charge of $2.50 plus $.50 for each check you wrote.

Alpha Bank

Monthly charge	**$2.50**
Check charges	
($.50 × 20 checks)	**+ 10.00**
Total service charge	**$12.50**

Use the Plan C chart to find your service charges in each of the other banks. Remember that your minimum balance was $399 and you wrote 20 checks.

3. Beta Bank

Monthly charge _____

Charge for 20 checks _____

Total charges _____

4. Gamma Bank

Monthly charge _____

Charge for 20 checks _____

Total charges _____

5. Delta Bank

Monthly charge _____

Charge for 20 checks _____

Total charges _____

Suppose your minimum balance was $863.97 and you wrote 25 checks. Find the service charges (if any) at each of the four banks.

6. Alpha Bank

Monthly charge _____

Charge for 25 checks _____

Total charges _____

7. Beta Bank

Monthly charge _____

Charge for 25 checks _____

Total charges _____

8. Gamma Bank

Monthly charge _____

Charge for 25 checks _____

Total charges _____

9. Delta Bank

Monthly charge _____

Charge for 25 checks _____

Total charges _____

When payday came around again, Bill went to Central Bank. He asked to see Nina. "I'm taking your advice," he told her. "How do I open a checking account?"

Nina showed him how to make out a **deposit slip.** Bill deposited his paycheck of $364.44. He also deposited $60 he had been carrying in his billfold.

Nina gave Bill a piece of paper. She said, "Here's your **receipt.** Always be sure to get a receipt when you put money in the bank." She gave Bill some blank checks that he could use right away. Later the bank sent him some checks with his name, address, phone number, and account number printed on them. He also received his **ATM** card.

```
┌─────────────────────────────────────────┐
│  ──────  Central Bank  ──────            │
│            24 Hour Teller                │
│                                          │
│              4 9 3 7 8 0                 │
│                                          │
│  WILLIAM P. ROSSI         12/97 to 12/98 │
└─────────────────────────────────────────┘
```

Bill asked Nina, "What is an ATM card?" Nina explained that sometimes Bill might want to go to the bank in the evening or on the weekend. But the bank isn't open during these times. Nina explained that many banks have an automated teller machine (ATM). An ATM is a computer-operated machine that Bill can use for deposits and **withdrawals** by using his ATM card. The ATM at Bill's bank operated 24 hours a day.

- You can get money from your account, even when the bank is closed.
- The lines at the teller machines are often shorter than those inside the bank.
- At some stores and gas stations, you can use your ATM card instead of writing a

| Words to Know | When Opening a Checking Account |

deposit slip: a piece of paper used to record the amount of money put into a bank account.

receipt: a piece of paper that shows how much money was received.

ATM: automatic teller machine. A computer-operated machine used for banking.

withdrawal: money that is taken from a bank account; or the act of taking money from a bank account.

account number: a special number the bank gives to a bank account.

code number: a number that shows which bank a check is drawn from.

currency: money in bills; cash.

personal checks: checks that have a person's name, address, sometimes a phone number, and an account number printed on them.

check register: a small book used to record the amount of money deposited in and taken out of a checking account.

check. The amount is subtracted from your account.

When Bill received the ATM card in the mail, he signed the back of it. The card had a number printed on the front. It also came with a four-number code that was not on the card. Bill will have to enter the code every time he uses the ATM. No one but Bill would know the code. This way, only Bill could use his card to take money from his account.

Here are some things to remember about using an ATM card.

- You cannot withdraw more money than you have in your account.
- You should never deposit cash.
- Most banks have a limit on the amount you can withdraw each day.

Look at Bill's deposit slip. He filled in these blanks:

1. The number 116 shows in which branch of Central Bank Bill deposited his money.

2. Every bank account has a special number. Bill's **account number** is 49-3780.

3. The American Bankers Association has a **code number** for each bank. Bill's employer has an account in bank number 11-37. Bill's paycheck is drawn on that account.

4. Bill deposited $60 in **currency.**

5. He deposited his paycheck, $364.44.

6. His total deposit was $424.44.

Bill's **personal checks** looked like the one shown. (He wrote this check for $21.95 to Marty's Menswear for a shirt.)

Bill also received a **check register** from his bank.

1	2	3

116	49-3780
BRANCH NO.	ACCOUNT NO.

William Rossi
NAME

2335 Aurora St.
ADDRESS

San Juan,   Calif.   95014
CITY   STATE   ZIP

1-26-97
DATE

Central Bank
San Juan, CA 95014

LIST CHECKS BY BANK NUMBER		DOLLARS			CENTS	
CURRENCY				6	0	00
COIN						
CHECKS 1 11-37			3	6	4	44
2						
3						
4						
SUB TOTAL						
TOTAL DEPOSIT			4	2	4	44

Bill's deposit slip.

William Rossi
2335 Aurora Street
San Juan, CA 95014

NUMBER 100

Feb. 16, 19 97

PAY TO THE ORDER OF _____ Marty's Menswear _____ $ 21.⁹⁵

Twenty-one and ⁹⁵/₁₀₀ _____ DOLLARS
non-negotiable

Central Bank
1554 Farris Avenue
San Juan, CA 95014
0815 011649 378 0

William Rossi

Bill's personal check.

PLEASE BE SURE TO **DEDUCT** ANY PER CHECK OR SERVICE CHARGE THAT MAY APPLY TO YOUR ACCOUNT.

1	2

CHECK NO.	DATE	CHECKS ISSUED TO OR DESCRIPTION OF DEPOSIT	AMOUNT OF CHECK	✔	AMOUNT OF DEPOSIT	BALANCE	
	1/26	Deposit			424 44	424	44
100	2/16	Marty's Menswear	21 95			402	49

3	4

A check register is a small book used to keep a record of deposits and checks. It should be kept up to date. Every deposit should be added to the balance. Every check should be subtracted from the balance. Every ATM deposit and withdrawal should be recorded. By keeping the register up to date, Bill always knew how much money he had in the bank.

Bill began his check register like this:

1. He recorded his first deposit, $424.44.

2. He recorded his balance, also $424.44.

3. He recorded his first check, $21.95, which he paid to Marty's Menswear for a shirt.

4. He subtracted $21.95 from $424.44. Then he recorded his new balance, $402.49.

PLEASE BE SURE TO **DEDUCT** ANY PER CHECK OR SERVICE CHARGE THAT MAY APPLY TO YOUR ACCOUNT.

CHECK NO.	DATE	CHECKS ISSUED TO OR DESCRIPTION OF DEPOSIT	AMOUNT OF CHECK		✔	AMOUNT OF DEPOSIT		BALANCE 1,632	25
	1/16	Deposit				225	00		
350	2/23	Cash	35	00					
351	2/25	Health Plan	85	76					
	2/25	Deposit				174	70		
352	2/26	Arts Auto Repair	66	53					
353	2/26	Telephone Company	20	65					
354	2/27	J. K. Supermarket	27	75					
355	2/27	ATM Withdrawal	20	00					
356	2/28	Evening News	9	50					
	2/28	Deposit				588	10		
357	2/28	Villa Rosa	500	00					

1. Fill out this check register. Add the deposits and subtract the checks. What is the balance at the end of February? _____

2. Record the following items on the check register. Then find the new balance. What is the new balance? _____

Check No.	Date	Check or Deposit	Amount
358	3/1	J. K. Supermarket	$30.41
359	3/3	Telephone Co.	18.97
360	3/3	Lifeline Insurance Co.	85.00
361	3/3	Dr. R. J. Paine	65.00
	3/4	ATM withdrawal	20.00
362	3/5	Frock Shoppe	107.98
	3/6	Deposit	198.75
363	3/9	J. K. Supermarket	22.92
364	3/11	Internal Revenue	400.00
365	3/12	Harry's Hardware	19.76
	3/15	ATM Deposit	515.00

PLEASE BE SURE TO **DEDUCT** ANY PER CHECK OR SERVICE CHARGE THAT MAY APPLY TO YOUR ACCOUNT.

CHECK NO.	DATE	CHECKS ISSUED TO OR DESCRIPTION OF DEPOSIT	AMOUNT OF CHECK	✔	AMOUNT OF DEPOSIT	BALANCE 731 02	

One Saturday afternoon Nina showed Bill her bank statement. "Central Bank will send you a statement like this every month," she said. "The bank will return your **canceled checks** along with the statement."

"After the bank pays the money for each check you write, the check is canceled. If the bank returns your canceled checks, you should save them. If you need a copy of a canceled check, ask the bank to send you one. You may need to use a canceled check, or a copy of it, to prove you have paid a bill."

Then she said, "Now I'll show you how **to balance** your checkbook." (Here, *checkbook* really means the check register.)

Bill sat down and looked at Nina's statement. He said, "The bank keeps track of everything—all the deposits, checks, and withdrawals. So why do I have to balance my checkbook?"

Words to Know	When Balancing a Checkbook

canceled checks: checks the bank has marked to show that they cannot be used again. The bank may send your canceled checks back to you.

to balance: to find out if two numbers are the same. The amount of money in your check register should be the same as the amount shown on your statement.

overdraw: to write checks for more money than you have in your checking account.

bounced check: a "bad check" that the bank returns to the person who tried to cash it. A check may "bounce" if you overdraw your account. To make the check good, you must put more money in your account right away.

outstanding: when a check has not been returned to the bank and does not appear on your bank statement.

"Do you ever make mistakes in arithmetic?" asked Nina.

"Sure," said Bill. "Doesn't everybody?"

"Even banks make mistakes," Nina said. "But you won't find the mistakes unless you balance your checkbook. If your arithmetic is wrong, you might **overdraw** your account. You might write checks for more money than you have in the bank. Then your checks will bounce. And every **bounced check** can cost you money."

"OK, OK!" said Bill. "I'll learn to balance my checkbook. I don't want to go to jail for writing bad checks."

"You probably wouldn't go to jail," said Nina. "Not unless you write bad checks on purpose! But Central Bank will charge you $15 for every bad check you write. And a lot of companies and stores charge a fee if you give them bad checks."

Here is Nina's statement.

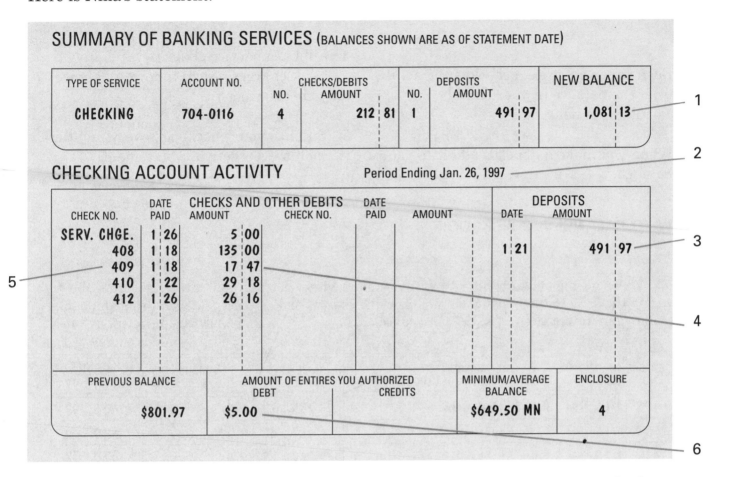

SUMMARY OF BANKING SERVICES (BALANCES SHOWN ARE AS OF STATEMENT DATE)

TYPE OF SERVICE	ACCOUNT NO.	NO.	CHECKS/DEBITS AMOUNT	NO.	DEPOSITS AMOUNT	NEW BALANCE
CHECKING	704-0116	4	212	81	1	491	97	1,081	13

— 1

— 2

CHECKING ACCOUNT ACTIVITY   Period Ending Jan. 26, 1997

CHECK NO.	DATE PAID	CHECKS AND OTHER DEBITS AMOUNT	CHECK NO.	DATE PAID	AMOUNT	DATE	DEPOSITS AMOUNT
SERV. CHGE.	1 26	5 00					
408	1 18	135 00				1 21	491 97
409	1 18	17 47					
410	1 22	29 18					
412	1 26	26 16					

— 3

— 4

PREVIOUS BALANCE	AMOUNT OF ENTIRES YOU AUTHORIZED DEBT	CREDITS	MINIMUM/AVERAGE BALANCE	ENCLOSURE
$801.97	$5.00		$649.50 MN	4

— 5

— 6

1. The bank's balance is $1,081.13. This amount should agree with the balance for January 26 in Nina's checkbook (if the bank canceled all her checks).

2. Nina's checks or deposits after January 26 are not listed on this statement.

3. Nina compares the deposits with the deposits she recorded in her checkbook. Usually these two numbers agree. What should you do if these numbers aren't the same?
   • Check your receipts from the bank.
   • Check your ATM receipts.
   • Look for a mistake in your checkbook.
   • If you did not make a mistake, ask the bank to check their records.

4. Next, Nina compares the amounts of the checks on her statement with the amounts she recorded in her check register. The numbers should be the same.

5. The checks listed by number on the statement have been canceled. That means the money has been taken from Nina's account. Is there a check missing from the list? If a check has not been returned to the bank it is **outstanding**. It should appear on the next statement.

6. Once a month, Nina subtracts the service charges from the last balance in her checkbook. (It doesn't matter when you subtract them. Just don't forget to do it!) But to balance her checkbook, Nina must subtract the service charges from the balance she had on the day the statement came out (January 26). You can see how this works on the next page.

Balancing a checkbook is not as hard as it looks. Nina gave Bill four tips to make it easy:

1. Each time you write a check, subtract it from the balance in your checkbook. A calculator is helpful.

2. When you make a deposit, add it to your balance.

3. Record all ATM transactions in your checkbook.

4. Subtract service charges—and any other bank charges—each time you balance your checkbook.

5. Balance your checkbook every month, as soon as you get your statement.

HOW TO BALANCE A CHECKBOOK

1. Make sure the amounts here are the same as the amount on your statements.

2. Put a mark after each check the bank has canceled.

3. Draw a line under the last check that the bank canceled.

CHECK NO.	DATE	CHECKS ISSUED TO OR DESCRIPTION OF DEPOSIT	AMOUNT OF CHECK		✔	AMOUNT OF DEPOSIT		BALANCE	
								801	97
408	1/16	Arts Auto Repair	135	00	✔			666	97
409	1/16	J. K. Supermarket	17	47	✔			649	50
410	1/20	Frock Shoppe	29	18	✔			620	32
	1/21	ATM Deposit				491	97	1112	29
411	1/22	Dr. Paine	50	00				1062	29
412	1/24	J. K. Supermarket	26	16	✔			1036	13
413	1/29	J. K. Supermarket	30	86				1005	27
414	1/31	Villa Rosa (Rent)	500	00				505	27
		Service Charge	5	00				500	27

4. Add to your balance any checks that do not appear on your statement. Check 411 was not canceled, so add $50.

$1036.13
+ 50.00
1086.13

5. Subtract the service charges
$1086.13
− 5.00
1081.13
This last amount should be the same as the balance on your statement.

NOTE
Here is the amount that must agree with the balance on your bank statement, once you've added any outstanding checks.

GOOD WORK, NINA!

Nina's checkbook balances. She kept good records and did not make any mistakes. She has subtracted the $5 service charge. Now she knows that her new balance—$1,081.13—is correct.

Here is another copy of Nina's checkbook—but in this copy there are two mistakes. Compare the two copies to find the mistakes.

1. The first mistake is in copying numbers. Circle the mistake and write a *1* beside it. Do not correct this mistake.

CHECK NO.	DATE	CHECKS ISSUED TO OR DESCRIPTION OF DEPOSIT	AMOUNT OF CHECK		✔	AMOUNT OF DEPOSIT		BALANCE	
								801	79
408	1/16	Arts Auto Repair	135	00	✔			666	79
409	1/16	J. K. Supermarket	17	47	✔			649	32
410	1/20	Frock Shoppe	29	18	✔			620	14
	1/21	ATM Deposit				491	97	1112	11
411	1/22	Dr. Paine	50	00				1062	11
412	1/24	J. K. Supermarket	26	16	✔			1045	95
413	1/29	J. K. Supermarket	30	86				1015	09
414	1/31	Villa Rosa (Rent)	500	00				515	09
		Service Charge	5	00				510	09

2. The second mistake is in subtraction. Circle this mistake in the balance column and write a *2* beside it. Do not correct this mistake, either.

3. Now correct the balance. Write *corrected balance* on the bottom line of the register. Then write the correct total in the balance column.

Consumer Tip

If you can't balance your checkbook, look at the ✔ column for the last several months. You may find a check that has never been cashed.

But suppose you've checked *everything* and you still can't balance your checkbook. Go to the bank for help. Take all your records: checkbook, deposit receipts, statements, and canceled checks.

After Bill opened his checking account, Central Bank sent him a letter. The letter said, "Open a savings account today. Get a free gift." It said the bank would give a free set of drinking glasses to anyone who opened a new savings account. Bill showed the letter to Jennifer.

"We could use the glasses after we get married," Jennifer said. "We can rent an apartment with furniture in it. But we'll have to buy our own dishes and glasses. Maybe I should open my savings account at Central Bank. Then I'd get a set of glasses free."

"But Nina said you'd get more interest at a savings and loan," Bill pointed out. "Let's ask Nina about this."

"OK," Jennifer said. "I'll ask Nina to have lunch with me tomorrow."

Later Jennifer called Nina. They made plans to meet for lunch. Then Jennifer told Nina about the money in her piggy bank. "I've been trying to save $25 a month," Jennifer said. "So far, I've saved about $225."

"Your money should be in a savings account," Nina said. "Tomorrow at lunch, I'll show you why."

The next day at lunch, Nina was ready to talk about saving. She took a paper out of her purse. Here is what she showed to Jennifer:

Piggy bank:	$25 a month = $300.00 a year = $1,500 in five years
Savings account at $2\frac{1}{2}$% interest:	$25 a month = $304.09 a year = $1,599.34 in five years

---

Words to Know	**When Opening a Savings Account**

interest rate: a percent that is paid on the money in a savings account.

insured savings: money in a savings account that is protected by the federal government.

principal: the money you deposit in a savings account. If you put $1,000 in the account, the principal is $1,000.

simple interest: interest paid on the principal. At $2\frac{1}{2}$%, you would earn $25 interest on $1,000 in a year. So at the end of the year, you would have $1,025.

compound interest: interest that is paid on the principal and also on the interest. With interest compounded daily at $2\frac{1}{2}$%, $1,000 would grow to $1,025.31 in one year's time.

"Wow!" said Jennifer. "I'd get $99 in interest! Just by saving $25 a month for five years!" Then Jennifer asked Nina about the glasses Central Bank was giving away. "The glasses are very pretty," Nina said. "But free gifts are not the most important thing to look for in a bank." Nina named three things to look for in a savings account:

1. A high **interest rate.** Jennifer could get only $2\frac{1}{4}$% interest from Central Bank. But she could get $2\frac{1}{2}$% from a savings and loan.

2. **Insured savings.** Savings are insured by FDIC—Federal Deposit Insurance Corporation. With FDIC, money is safer because the U.S. government stands behind it.

3. Interest compounded daily. Jennifer will get **compound interest** on the $225 that she deposits in her account. And she will get *more* interest on the interest itself, since it adds up every day. When only **simple interest** is paid on the **principal,** your money earns less than when it is compounded daily.

$2\frac{1}{2}$% Growth through monthly savings plus compounding interest.

	1 YEAR	2 YEARS	3 YEARS	4 YEARS	5 YEARS	6 YEARS	10 YEARS
Save each month $ 25	304.10	615.89	935.56	1,263.33	1,599.39	1,943.95	3,411.60
Save each month $ 50	608.19	1,231.77	1,871.13	2,526.66	3,198.77	3,887.90	6,823.19
Save each month $100	1,216.38	2,463.54	3,742.25	5,053.31	6,397.54	7,775.79	13,646.38

Use this chart to answer questions about compound interest.

1. a. Suppose you deposit $25 each month for three years. How much money will you deposit during this time? _____

   b. Now check the chart. How much interest will your money earn in three years? _____

2. a. Suppose you deposit $25 each month for five years. How much will you deposit during this time? _____

   b. Now check the chart again. How much interest will your money earn in five years? _____

3. a. Suppose you deposit $50 each month for two years. How much will you deposit during this time? _____

   b. How much interest will your money earn in two years? _____

4. a. Suppose you deposit $50 each month for four years. How much will you deposit during this time? _____

   b. How much interest will your money earn in four years? _____

5. a. Suppose you deposit $100 every month for one year. How much will you deposit during this time? _____

   b. How much interest will your money earn in one year? _____

6. a. Suppose you deposit $100 each month for ten years. How much will you deposit during this time? _____

   b. How much interest will your money earn in ten years? _____

"Everyone should have a savings account," Nina said. "The less money you have, the more you need a savings account to fall back on."

Then Nina told Jennifer this story: "When I was 17, my dog was hit by a car. She needed an operation that cost $200. I couldn't ask my parents for the money because my dad had been sick for a long time. The vet said he could put my dog to sleep! But I didn't want my dog to die!"

"What did you do?" Jennifer asked.

"I used my savings," Nina answered. "I had a summer job waiting on tables. I had saved more than $200 from my tips. So my dog had an operation and got well."

"I see what you mean," Jennifer said. "Everyone needs a savings account, just in case something happens. Something that you didn't plan on. Something really bad that costs a lot of money."

"Yes," said Nina, "but that's not the only way that savings help. Many people save money for something special. Jose wanted to buy a secondhand car. It isn't easy to find a good one. Jose looked for a long time. While he was looking, his money was earning interest in a savings account."

Later that day, Jennifer opened a savings account at National Savings and Loan. She deposited $225. Jennifer was saving for "something special." When she and Bill were married, she could buy things for their home.

Consumer Tip

Most savings and loan companies have more than one savings plan. Each plan may pay a different interest rate. Usually, the longer you agree to keep your money in the account, the more interest the company will pay you. When you open your savings account, ask questions. Get the best savings plan you can.

One year Jose paid too much income tax. Last year he got back a check for $848.63. He put the money in his account at National Savings and Loan.

Jose wanted to buy a car. While he looked for a car to buy, his money earned interest. At last he found a car that was just right. He used $1,500 of his savings as the down payment.

National Savings gives a **passbook** to each person who opens an account. The passbook is used for keeping records.

Here is Jose's passbook. It shows the money Jose deposited and the interest that was paid. Then it shows a **withdrawal:** Jose took $1,500 out of his account.

Banking Words	
passbook: a small book that shows the amount of money put in and taken out of a savings account.	
withdrawal: money taken out of a savings account.	

DATE	WITHDRAWAL	DEPOSIT	INTEREST	BALANCE
JUN 30			4.09	656.92
JUN 30		$848.63		
SEP 30			9.44	
DEC 31			9.50	
MAR 30			9.56	
APR 1	$1,500.00			

1. Fill in the balance column. Add the interest and the deposit. Subtract the withdrawal. How much is the balance in Jose's account on April 1? _____

1. With a regular savings account, you can deposit or withdraw money any time. How can a savings account help people who lose their jobs? How can it help people who have no health insurance? Can you think of other ways that people use their savings?

2. Service charges are not the same at all banks. Compare service charges for the banks in your city. Find out the minimum balance set by each bank. Could you get a free checking account in any of these banks?

3. Often savings and loan companies give free services to people who deposit $1,000 or more. Visit one of these companies. Ask about free services. Then tell the class what you have learned.

4. Look into other savings plans at local banks. Mutual Funds and CDs (certificates of deposit) are types of savings plans. Ask, "How long do I have to keep my money in the account? What risks are involved?"

TEST YOURSELF

In each problem find out how much simple interest a deposit would earn at $2\frac{1}{2}\%$ ($2\frac{1}{2}\% = .025$). You may use a calculator.

Example:
$\begin{array}{r} \$550 \text{ deposit} \\ \times\ .025\ \ 2\frac{1}{2}\% \text{ interest} \\ \hline 2750 \\ 1100 \\ \hline \$13.750 = \$13.75 \text{ (rounded off)} \end{array}$

1.
$\begin{array}{r} \$225 \\ \times\ .025 \\ \hline \end{array}$

2.
$\begin{array}{r} \$788 \\ \times\ .025 \\ \hline \end{array}$

3.
$\begin{array}{r} \$1978.50 \\ \times\ .025 \\ \hline \end{array}$

4.
$\begin{array}{r} \$319.77 \\ \times\ .025 \\ \hline \end{array}$

5.
$\begin{array}{r} \$456.56 \\ \times\ .025 \\ \hline \end{array}$

6.
$\begin{array}{r} \$2033 \\ \times\ .025 \\ \hline \end{array}$

How much does a checking account cost? Use this chart to find out how much each person paid for service charges in one month.

Plan C Service Charges

Minimum Daily Balance	Under $500	$500–$999	$1,000–$1,999	$2,000 or more
Monthly charge	$3.00	$5.00	$10.00	NO SERVICE CHARGE
Charge per check	.50	.25	no charge	

7. Anne's minimum balance was $829. She wrote 13 checks. _____

8. Andy's minimum balance was $187. He wrote 18 checks. _____

9. Audrey's minimum balance was $2,163.97. She wrote 20 checks. _____

10. Alan's minimum balance was $602.44. He wrote 22 checks. _____

ANSWERS:
1. $5.63 2. $19.70 3. $49.46 4. $7.99 5. $11.41 6. $50.83 7. $8.25 8. $12 9. 0 (no charge) 10. $10.50

Match these two lists. Write the letter of the correct word in each blank.

Words		Meanings
A. balance	_____	1. a company that lends money and pays interest on savings
B. deposit		
	_____	2. a paper that shows deposits, checks, and the balance in a checking account
C. statement		
D. service charge	_____	3. a fee paid for the use of money
E. withdrawal	_____	4. an amount of money taken out of a savings account
F. interest	_____	5. to write a check for more money than you have in your account
G. overdraw		
	_____	6. the amount of money in a bank account at any time
H. passbook		
	_____	7. an amount of money put into a bank account
I. savings and loan association	_____	8. a U.S. corporation that insures bank accounts
J. FDIC	_____	9. a fee that you pay to a bank for taking care of your money and paying your checks
	_____	10. record of deposits, withdrawals, and interest in a savings account

Mark each sentence T for true or F for false.

_____ 11. Banks never pay interest on money in checking accounts.

_____ 12. Compound interest pays less than simple interest.

_____ 13. Banks pay interest on all checking accounts.

_____ 14. Checks "bounce" if you overdraw your account.

_____ 15. You should balance your checkbook only once a year.

ANSWERS:

11. F   12. F   13. F   14. T   15. F
1. I   2. C   3. F   4. E   5. G   6. A   7. B   8. J   9. D   10. H

Finding a Place to Live

Preview: Apartments for Rent

Read the ads under "Apartments—Furnished." Notice the abbreviations. (An abbreviation is the short way to write a word.) In the blanks below tell what these abbreviations mean.

Apartments—Furnished

ALMADEN Exp. 1 br., quiet, util. paid. $535. 555-0926

FOUNTAIN PARK, 1, 2, Br. from $465. 555-1000. 1026 Midvale

DOWNTOWN $565. Cln. 1 bdrm. W/G pd. 470 N. 34th St., aft. 5

DOWNTOWN 1 bdrm. Parking. Refers. $415. 555-3100. Agent

DOWNTOWN—No. 4th St. 1 bdrm., partly furn. $495/mo. 555-0577 or 555-1797 aft. 5 p.m.

SO. 15th St. 1 Bdrm. Clean. $520. 555-1327

STATE UNIVERSITY: 3½ rms. No pets. $410 on lease. Apply 421 East St.

VALLEY MEDICAL Center. 1 br. clean. No pets. $465. Aft. 4 p.m. 555-5592

WESTSIDE, lrg. studio, AEK, incl. DW, ww cpts. incl. Kit/ba. pool & port. No pets. Quiet living. 555-1438

WESTSIDE, spac. Jr. 1 br. W&G pd. A/C. No pets. $415. 555-6034

WILLOW GLEN AREA
Clean   Quiet
1 & 2 Br. furn. only w/garden court. Conven. loc. to 280 & 17. Pool; air, dishw. or patio. Starting $498. 555-6991

NEAT CLEAN & QUIET 1 br., nr. Valley Med. Cntr. $465. 555-0899.

ATTRACTIVE furn. 1 br., shag cpts, immac. No pets. $480. 1089 N. 5th. 555-8711

1 BR. $510. W&G pd., carport. Quiet area. 555-3852, 555-3937

1. 1 br. _____

2. util. paid _____

3. cln. 1 bdrm. _____

4. W/G pd. _____

5. partly furn. _____

6. aft. 5 p.m. _____

7. 3½ rms. _____

8. AEK incl. DW _____

9. ww cpts. _____

10. air, dishw. _____

ANSWERS:
1. one bedroom 2. utilities paid 3. clean one bedroom
4. water and gas paid 5. partly furnished 6. after 5 p.m.
7. 3½ rooms 8. all-electric kitchen, including dishwasher
9. wall-to-wall carpets 10. air-conditioning, dishwasher

Finding a Place to Live

"Why wait?" asked Bill. "If we can find a place to live, let's get married right away."

"We are taking home almost $260 a week," Jennifer said. "Let's look for an apartment that rents for $260 a month or less."

"Who cares if it's small?" Bill asked. "We can move to a bigger place next summer."

"By then I'll have a full-time job," Jennifer said.

"And I'll get a pay raise," Bill added.

On Saturday Jennifer and Bill borrowed a car from Jennifer's mother. They wanted to drive around and look at apartments. But first they drew a big circle on the city map. The warehouse where Bill worked was at the top of the circle. The TV repair shop where Jennifer worked was at the bottom. They wanted to find an apartment somewhere inside the circle. The best place would be halfway between the warehouse and the TV shop. And it had to be near a bus stop. So they drew the bus routes on the map.

Words to Know	**When Finding a Place to Live**

landlord: a person who owns a building and rents it to others.

utilities: services such as gas, electricity, water, and garbage pickup. Either the landlord or the tenant must pay for these services.

lease: a contract between a landlord and a tenant.

deposit: extra money (besides the rent) that the tenant pays before moving into a building. Some deposits are returned to the tenant when the tenant moves out. For example, a key deposit is returned when the tenant gives the key back to the landlord.

tenant: a person who rents an apartment.

rental agreement: any terms that the landlord and tenant agree to. The terms may be written and signed like a lease, or they may be oral (agreed upon by talking).

evicted: forced to move out of a building. For example, a landlord can evict a tenant who does not pay the rent.

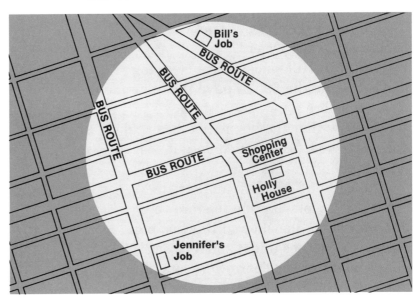

By now Bill knew the city very well. He knew all the main streets because he drove a delivery truck. He knew where to find apartments. Bill knew which streets were clean and quiet. These streets were also well lighted at night. Such streets would be the best places to live.

Bill drove to a big, old house on a corner in a good part of town. There was a sign on the house:

FOR RENT
1-BEDROOM APARTMENT

Jennifer and Bill knocked on the door and met the **landlord,** Mr. Hill. Mr. and Mrs. Hill lived on the first floor of the house. There were apartments on the second and third floors. Mr. Hill showed Jennifer and Bill the apartment on the top floor. They had to climb two sets of stairs.

They saw three big rooms and a bath. The apartment was clean, but the rooms were hot. The furniture looked strong, but it was not very pretty.

"The rent is $420 a month," Mr. Hill said. "We pay for all the **utilities.** You don't have to sign a **lease.** Just write me a check for one month's rent, plus a $95 **deposit.** Then you can move in any time."

Jennifer asked, "Do we get our deposit back when we move out?"

"No," Mr. Hill said. "It is a cleaning deposit. I use the $95 to have the apartment cleaned before a new **tenant** moves in."

Bill saw that the phone had been taken out. He asked, "How much does it cost to have a phone put in?"

"About $35," Mr. Hill answered.

"There is lots of room to store things," Jennifer said. She showed Bill two big closets for clothes and a small closet for sheets and towels. There were lots of cupboards in the kitchen.

"We will have to buy dishes and pots and pans," Jennifer said. "And we'll have to buy our own sheets and towels."

"And there's no TV set," Bill said.

"You can bring your own TV set, if you want one," Mr. Hill said. "But you have to turn it off at 10 o'clock at night. That's part of the **rental agreement.** The last tenant was **evicted** because he broke the agreement. His TV kept me awake every night."

Jennifer said, "Maybe we should look at some more apartments before we make up our minds." Bill thanked Mr. Hill and said good-bye.

Outside, Jennifer said, "That place costs too much."

"Who cares?" Bill asked. "Who wants to live with a fussy man who can throw us out if we watch the 11 o'clock news on TV!"

1. A tenant moved into Mr. Hill's apartment and had a phone put in. How much did the tenant have to pay for everything before moving in?

_____ rent

_____ deposit

_____ phone

_____ total

2. Every apartment has both good points and bad points. What do you think Jennifer and Bill would *like* about Mr. Hill's apartment?

a. _____

b. _____

c. _____

d. _____

e. _____

3. What do you think Bill and Jennifer would *not like* about Mr. Hill's apartment?

a. _____

b. _____

c. _____

d. _____

e. _____

Jennifer and Bill drove to a place called Woodland Park. Woodland Park was a "garden apartment"—many buildings with grass and trees around them. There was a big sign near the street:

NOW RENTING—FROM $410
Furnished or Unfurnished
Studios
One-Bedroom
Two-Bedrooms

Words to Know **When Renting an Apartment**

manager: a person who takes care of a building for the landlord.

security deposit: extra money a tenant pays before moving into a building. The landlord uses this money to pay for anything tenants break in the apartment. If the tenants leave the apartment in good shape, they get their security deposit back.

Bill and Jennifer found the **manager,** Mrs. Lopez. They asked to see a furnished studio.

Mrs. Lopez said, "I can show you a studio that rents for $480."

"But the sign says $410," said Jennifer.

"Yes," said Mrs. Lopez, "we have a few studios that rent for $410. But they are all rented. They cost less because they are on the main street. You get some noise there from big trucks and buses that go by. But we have other studios on the inside where it's quiet. Inside studios rent for $480."

Jennifer and Bill followed Mrs. Lopez down a sidewalk and up some stairs. The studio was one room with two sofas that could be made into beds. For eating, there was a counter with two stools. Behind the counter was a tiny kitchen.

The studio seemed dark because it had only one window. The room was not too hot or too cold. But Bill thought it might get too hot in the summer. One window would not let in enough air.

Everything in the studio was new and clean. Jennifer liked the colors—mostly blue and gold with off-white walls. But the walls were not very thick. They could hear music from the next apartment.

Mrs. Lopez showed them the bathroom and one big closet. Then she explained the lease.

The tenants had to sign a lease for six months. That means they would have to pay the rent for six months, even if they moved out before six months were over. But the landlord could not ask them to move—or raise the rent—for six months.

When tenants signed the lease, they had to pay two months' rent and a deposit of $200. When they moved out, they could get the deposit back if they left the studio in good shape. This fee is called a **security deposit.** If the tenants broke something, the landlord would use their deposit to replace it.

The studio had an electric stove and electric heat. If Jennifer and Bill lived at Woodland Park, they would pay for their own electricity. In the summer, when the heat was off, it might cost $12 a month or less. But in the winter, the electric bill might go up to $40 or more. The tenants would have to pay to start phone service. The landlord paid for the other utilities.

Bill said, "We're not ready to sign a lease. We want to think it over."

Later Jennifer said, "We can't even afford a nice studio apartment! We'll have to wait until next summer. Then I'll be out of school, and I can work full time."

"And I'll get a raise," said Bill.

EXERCISE 15

1. Suppose Bill and Jennifer rented a studio at Woodland Park for $410 a month. How much would they have to pay when they signed the lease?

   rent (two months)   _____

   security deposit   _____

   total   _____

2. Ms. Lupico rents a studio at Woodland Park. Here are her electric bills for the last six months of the year:

July	$10.20
August	$11.40
September	$11.28
October	$18.38
November	$29.35
December	$38.32

   a. How much did Ms. Lupico pay for electricity during these six months?   _____

   b. How much was her average electric bill? You may use a calculator.   _____

3. A tenant in Mr. Hill's house pays $420 a month for rent. Mr. Hill pays for utilities.

Ms. Lupico pays $410 a month at Woodland Park. She pays her own electric bill.

Check the apartment that costs more per year.

☐ The Hill House ☐ Woodland Park

4. What do you think Jennifer and Bill would *like* about the studio at Woodland Park?

a. _____

b. _____

c. _____

d. _____

e. _____

5. What do you think Jennifer and Bill would *not like* about the studio at Woodland Park?

a. _____

b. _____

c. _____

d. _____

e. _____

"Let's go see Sue Takata," Jennifer said. "Sue is moving into an apartment on Kemp Road. I have the address right here. Let's take a look." On the way to Kemp Road, Jennifer told Bill about her friend Sue.

"Sue came to San Juan about three months ago. She has been living with her cousins and looking for a place of her own. Last week she found a nice furnished apartment. She asked me to come to see it."

They found Sue at home. But her new apartment looked like a warehouse! It was full of paper bags and boxes. The bags were filled with groceries. The boxes were filled with things that every apartment needs. Sue had a good job. She had saved her money to buy these things for her new home.

Jennifer and Bill helped Sue unpack the bags and boxes. "It must cost a lot of money to start your own apartment," Jennifer said sadly.

"Yes, it does," Sue answered. "I bought almost all these things on sale—even the food. But the bills add up to quite a lot. I'll show you the bills. Then you'll have an idea how much it costs."

"We wanted to get married right away," Bill said. "But it looks as if we'll have to wait."

"Why don't you set a date for your wedding?" Sue asked. "Maybe setting the date will cheer you up."

"How about the Fourth of July?" Bill asked Jennifer.

"Why do you want to get married on July Fourth?" Jennifer asked.

"Then we'll never have to work on our anniversary," said Bill. "And all our friends will get the day off, too."

Jennifer laughed, but she liked that idea. "OK," she said. "Let's plan on it."

ALARM CLOCK

Reg. $9.99

$7.99

PILLOW

DACRON POLYESTER-FILLED BED PILLOWS

Reg. $8.99

$4.99

NO-IRON SHEETS

POLY-COTTON BROWN OR GREEN CASES $11.99 A PAIR

SHEETS—REG. $11.25
PILLOWCASES—REG. $12.62 pr.

$10.99

Sue bought these items for her bedroom.

1. How much did she pay for these items on sale?

2. How much would she have to pay for them at regular prices?

SALE		REGULAR
_____	alarm clock	_____
_____	2 pillows	_____
_____	2 blankets	_____
_____	4 sheets	_____
_____	4 pillowcases	_____
_____	1 bedspread	_____
_____	TOTAL	_____

3. How much did Sue save by buying these items on sale?

regular price   _____

sale price   _____

savings   _____

STITCHLESS-QUILTED SPREAD

MACHINE WASH, NO-IRON LARGER SIZES, MATCHING DRAPERIES ALSO ON SALE

20% OFF
REG. $40.00

$32.00

LUXURY BLANKET

DRESS YOUR BED IN OUR LOOM WOVEN BLANKET MILDEW RESISTANT MACHINE WASHABLE

REG. $38.69

$21.99

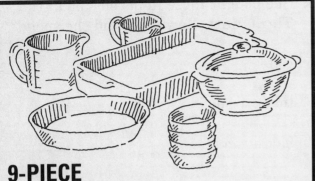

9-PIECE BAKING SET

1½-QT. COVERED CASSEROLE
2-QT. OBLONG BAKE DISH
1-QT. MEASURING CUP
4–8-OZ. CUSTARD CUPS
9" PIE PLATE

$26.91

4. Sue bought these items for her kitchen. How much did she pay for these five sets?

baking set _____

stainless steel flatware _____

stoneware dishes _____

6 kitchen tools _____

cookware _____

TOTAL _____

SPECIAL!

$19.99

Stainless steel flatware . . . 50-pc. services for 8. Each service for 8 includes 8 each: knives, forks, salad forks, soup spoons, 16 teaspoons, 1 butter knife, 1 sugar spoon.

SPECIAL!
$1 ea.

Handy kitchen tools with wood handles. Choose: slotted spoon, fork, masher, turner, ladle, basting spoon.

SPECIAL!

$16.88

20-pc. service for four stoneware set. Dishwasher and oven safe, chip resistant. Includes 4 ea.: soup bowls, cups, saucers, salad and dinner plates. Choice of 5 brightly colored patterns. Limited quantites.

46% off Cook Ware 7-pc. set

If purchased separately would be $84

$69.99

Set includes 1½, 2½-qt. covered sauce pans, 4½-qt. covered Dutch Oven, 9" open skillet (Oven cover fits).

TOOTHPASTE
WITH 12¢ OFF ON LABEL

REDUCED PRICE

$1.49

COFFEE
**2 LB. TIN
ALL GRINDS**

EA.
$3.49

DETERGENT

5 LB. 4 OZ.
$4.19

5. Sue bought these items on sale at the Thrift Mart. How much did she spend?

coffee _____

toilet tissue _____

baking soda _____

cleanser _____

toothpaste _____

detergent _____

2 bars soap _____

sugar _____

dust pan _____

TOTAL _____

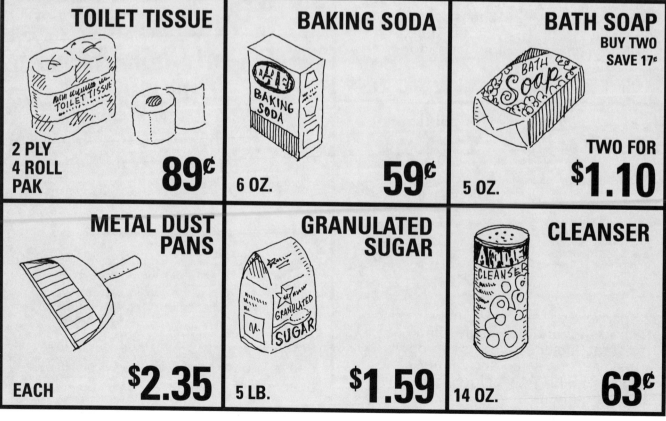

TOILET TISSUE

2 PLY
4 ROLL
PAK
89¢

BAKING SODA

6 OZ.
59¢

BATH SOAP
**BUY TWO
SAVE 17¢**

TWO FOR
5 OZ. **$1.10**

METAL DUST PANS

EACH **$2.35**

GRANULATED SUGAR

5 LB. **$1.59**

CLEANSER

14 OZ. **63¢**

VINEGAR
32 OZ.

85¢

TEA BAGS

$1.79

PEPPER

EACH **$2.29**

SALT

EACH **69¢**

CHERRY KITCHEN TERRY ENSEMBLES

Towel. reg. $1.79 . . . . $1.43
Oven Mitt, reg. $1.79 . . . . $1.43
Pot Holder, reg. 89¢ . . . . 71¢
Dishcloth, reg. 89¢ . . . . 71¢

20% OFF

RICE

$1.59

BAKING POWDER

63¢

POTATOES

10 LB. **$1.39**

FLOUR

5 LB. **95¢**

6. Sue bought these items at the Super Saver Market. How much did she spend?

flour   _____

salt   _____

pepper   _____

potatoes   _____

rice   _____

baking powder   _____

tea bags   _____

vinegar   _____

3 dish towels   _____

3 dish cloths   _____

2 oven mitts   _____

2 pot holders   _____

TOTAL   _____

7. How much did Sue spend on everything for her new apartment?

    a. items for her bedroom   _____

    b. items for her kitchen   _____

    c. items from the Thrift Mart   _____

    d. items from the Super Saver Market   _____

    e. TOTAL   _____

    Sue found her apartment on February 20. But she was not ready to move in yet. She asked the manager to hold the apartment for her until March 1.

    "That means the apartment will be empty for eight more days," the manager said. "I'll hold the apartment for you. But you have to pay eight days' rent as a deposit."

    Sue gave the manager a check for eight days' rent. He kept the apartment empty until March 1.

8. Sue's apartment rents for $518 a month. There are 28 days in February. How much is one day's rent?   _____

9. How much is eight days' rent?   _____

10. On March 1 Sue signed her lease. She had to pay these costs: one month's rent, a $195 security deposit, and a $5 key deposit. How much did Sue pay on March 1?   _____

11. Sue did not buy any fresh food—such as meat, milk, eggs, or vegetables. She forgot to buy a coffee maker. Can you think of other items she will need? List six items here:

    _____   _____

    _____   _____

    _____   _____

RENTING AN APARTMENT

On June 26 Bill got a telephone call from Jose. "I've found an apartment I think you'll like," Jose said. "It's on the first floor of our building. The tenants are moving out today. I saw their moving van. So I called you right away."

Bill liked the building where Jose and Nina lived. It was called Holly House. "How much is the rent?" Bill asked.

"I'm not sure," Jose said. "Nina and I pay $510 a month. But we have a lease. We may have to pay more when our lease runs out next month. We've heard that rents are going up."

Bill called Jennifer. "Let's meet at Jose's apartment after work," he said.

"That's a good idea," said Jennifer. "We can find out how long it takes for each of us to get there by bus."

At Holly House, Jennifer and Bill met the managers, Mr. and Mrs. Anderson. Mr. Anderson showed them apartment #9. There were many things that Bill and Jennifer liked about the apartment:

- It had a big living room with a dining area. The bedroom, bathroom, and kitchen were small. But there were two big closets for storage.
- Holly House was on a bus route. Both Bill and Jennifer could get to work by bus in less than an hour.
- It was near a shopping center. They could walk to a food market.
- Holly House had its own laundry room. It would be easy to wash clothes.
- Nina and Jose said the Andersons were good managers. They kept the building in good shape.

There were a few things that Jennifer and Bill did not like:

- Holly House was ten years old. The stove and refrigerator were still good. But some of the furniture was getting worn out.
- The street was not very quiet because a lot of people came to the shopping center.
- The rent had gone up to $520. The landlord paid for the water and garbage pickup. But the tenants had to pay their own gas and electric bills.

Jennifer was out of school now. She was working full time at the TV repair shop. She was now earning $7.50 an hour. Bill knew he would get a raise on July 1. Together, they would earn about $580 a week. Both Jennifer and Bill had money in their bank accounts. Now they felt that they could pay $520 a month.

Bill and Jennifer agreed to rent the apartment at Holly House. Mr. Anderson said it would be cleaned and ready to live in by July 1.

Jennifer and Bill read their lease with care before they signed it. Here are some of the terms of their lease:

- The lease lasted for six months. Jennifer and Bill had to pay rent for at least six months. After that, they could move out any time.
- But they had to give 30 days' notice before they moved. That means that they must let the managers know their plans at least a month before moving day.

- They could not sublet their apartment—that is, they could not move out and rent the apartment to someone else.
- They would get their security deposit back if they gave 30 days' notice and left the apartment in good shape.
- Tenants were not allowed to have water beds. (Many leases have special terms such as this.)
- Tenants were not allowed to have pets.

EXERCISE 17

1. Jennifer and Bill paid $520 rent, a $100 security deposit, and a $5 key deposit. How much did they pay for all these things? _____

2. Suppose they want to move out of Holly House. They give 30 days' notice. They return the key and leave the apartment in good shape. How much of their deposit money should they get back? _____

3. Both Jennifer and Bill will go to work by bus. They will use the city buses to go to other places also. Each ride costs 75 cents.

    But each person can buy a pass every month. There are two kinds of passes. A $15 pass is good for 22 bus rides. A $27 pass is good for any number of rides.

    Put an X beside the plan that will cost Jennifer and Bill the least:

    a. 75 cents a ride _____

    b. a $15 pass for 22 rides _____

    c. a $27 pass for any number of rides _____

Jennifer and Bill never had their own telephones before. Since they had no credit history, they had to pay a $95 deposit to start telephone service. Later they could get their deposit back—with interest—if they kept a good **credit record.** To get a good credit record, they would have to pay their phone bill on time every month.

How much does it cost to have a telephone? In some cities, even **local calls** cost money. The cost is up to you. You can keep the cost down if you:

- choose a low-cost monthly service plan.
- choose your long-distance carrier carefully.
- try not to make **long-distance calls.**

You can learn more about telephone service just by reading your phone book. If you need more help, call the phone company and ask questions. Get the facts *before* you order phone service. Then you will know what kind of service to ask for.

Many years ago, people had to get their phones from the telephone company. Now all kinds of stores sell phones. You can buy a phone for less than $20—or more than $100. Just look at some phones in a store and pick the one you want.

Words to Know	**About Telephone Service**

credit record: the good record a consumer earns by paying bills on time, or the bad record a consumer earns by not paying bills on time.

local calls: telephone calls to places in your own city or area.

long-distance calls: telephone calls to places in other cities or areas.

Consumer Tip

You can save money by calling during evening, night, and weekend hours. There are also discount rates during holidays. All this is explained in the phone book. Read your phone book to save money!

1. Jennifer and Bill bought a touch-tone phone and ordered phone service. Here are the charges they had to pay:

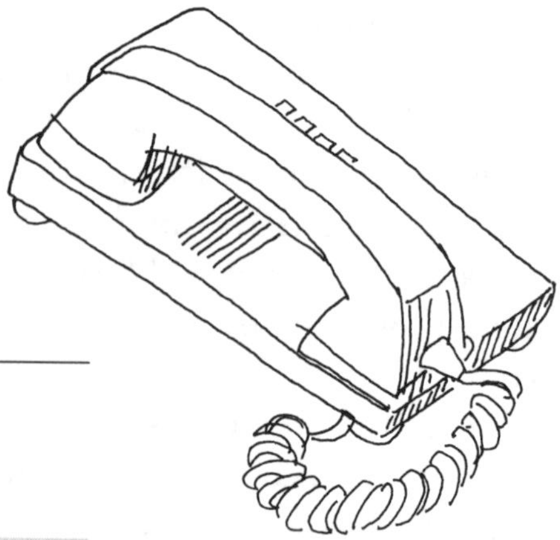

   $95.00 deposit

   $34.50 new order

   How much did they pay?   _____

   Their telephone company has three kinds of services:

   Plan A: Unlimited—any number of $21.25 a month
   local calls each month

   Plan B: Limited—60 local calls a month $13.45 a month

   Plan C: Limited—30 local calls a month $10.50 a month

2. How much does Plan A cost in one year?   _____

3. How much does Plan B cost in one year?   _____

4. How much does Plan C cost in one year?   _____

Jennifer and Bill ordered Service Plan B. They thought their phone bill would be only $13.45 a month. But when their first bill came, they saw some extra charges. They would have to pay these same charges every month.

5. Here are the charges on their first phone bill. How much did they pay all together? _____

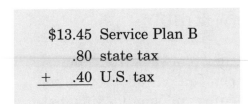

$13.45 Service Plan B
.80 state tax
+ .40 U.S. tax

6. Jennifer and Bill now had to choose a long-distance plan. They chose a company that provided free monthly service and had low rates to the places they normally called. Their long-distance phone bill was separate from their local phone bill.

   Here are their long-distance charges for one month. How much did they pay for long-distance calls all together? _____

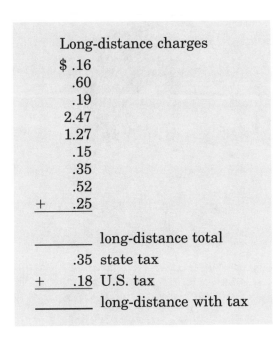

Long-distance charges
$ .16
.60
.19
2.47
1.27
.15
.35
.52
+ .25

_____ long-distance total
.35 state tax
+ .18 U.S. tax
_____ long-distance with tax

7. How much did they pay all together? _____

_____ Service Plan B with tax
+ _____ long-distance with tax
_____ total phone bill

1. Here are some items to check before you rent an apartment: Is the street well lighted? Is the building clean? Is there enough hot water? Can you see any signs of leaking pipes or bugs? What are some other items you would check? What questions would you ask the landlord or manager?

2. The United States has a law against unfair housing practices. The law says that a landlord must treat all people the same way. A landlord cannot turn anyone away because of race or color. Has anyone in your class had a problem with unfair housing practices? If so, find out how to take action against unfair landlords. Call Legal Aid or the housing authority of your city. Or call the U.S. Department of Housing and Urban Development (HUD).

3. Cut out "for rent" ads from your newspaper. Cut out ads from other nearby cities and small towns, too. Choose places big enough for yourself or for your family. Compare the rents. Where are the highest rents? Where are the lowest rents? Which areas have bus service? Does any area have a high crime rate? Which areas are safe places to live?

TEST YOURSELF

1. Jennifer earns $7.50 an hour. How much does she earn in a 40-hour week? _____

2. Bill started his job at $6.00 an hour. After six months, he got a $1.00 raise. What is his new hourly rate? _____

3. How much does Bill earn in a 40-hour week at his new rate? _____

4. How much do Bill and Jennifer earn together every week? _____

5. The average American family pays at least one week's income per month on rent. Jennifer and Bill will pay $520 a month for rent. Will they pay more or less than one week's income (before taxes) for rent? _____

6. Sue Takata paid $518 for rent when she moved into her apartment. She also paid a $195 security deposit and a $5 key deposit. Before she moved out, she gave 30 days' notice. She returned the key and left the apartment in good shape. How much deposit money should she get back? _____

7. Jennifer wanted to make a long-distance call to Michigan. She checked with the long-distance carrier and found out she could save up to 60% by calling before 8:00 A.M. The first minute costs 23 cents and each additional minute costs 19 cents. If she talks for ten minutes, how much will the call cost? _____

8. If Jennifer calls Michigan during business hours, she will pay 30 cents per minute. How much will a ten-minute call cost? _____

ANSWERS:

1. $300 2. $7.00 3. $280 4. $580 5. less 6. $200 7. $1.94 8. $3.00

Here is a list of ten words. Pick the right word for each sentence. Fill in the blanks.

cleaning	sublet	security
manager	tenant	landlord
deposit	lease	utilities
	evicted	

1. A _____
is a person who rents an apartment or a house.

2. The _____
is the person who owns the building and rents it to others.

3. The _____
takes care of the building for the owner.

4. A _____
is a contract between a landlord and a tenant.

5. Tenants can be _____
if they do not pay the rent.

6. A key _____
is returned to the tenant when the tenant returns the key
to the landlord.

7. To _____
means to move out of an apartment and rent it to someone
else.

8. A _____
deposit can be used to fix anything that the tenant breaks
or ruins.

9. A _____
deposit is never returned to the tenant. It is used to clean
the apartment after the tenant moves out.

10. _____
are services, such as gas, water, electricity, and garbage
pickup.

CHAPTER 5

Managing Money

Preview: The Family Budget

Here is a list of expenses for a family of four: mother, father, and two children. Their total budget for one year added up to $28,000. The list shows how much they spent for each item in the budget.

Find out what *percentage* they spent for each item. Divide each number by $28,000. You may use a calculator.

Example:

$$28,000)\overline{7560.00}$$

```
            .27
28,000)7560.00
        5600.0
        196000
        196000
             0
```

Item	Total in $	Percentage
1. Food	$7,560	27%
2. Housing	$8,960	_____
3. Transportation	$3,080	_____
4. Clothing	$2,520	_____
5. Utilities	$ 840	_____
6. Health Care	$2,240	_____
7. Household and Personal Needs	$1,680	_____
8. Recreation	$1,120	_____

ANSWERS:

2. 32%   3. 11%   4. 9%   5. 3%   6. 8%   7. 6%   8. 4%

Managing Money

And so Jennifer and Bill were married. They took a short wedding trip. Then they moved into apartment #9 at Holly House.

There were lots of new things—mostly wedding presents—in their apartment. And Jennifer's mother had given them her old TV set. But they still needed many things—like more towels and more pots and pans.

Now they had to change the names on their bank accounts. Jennifer's name was added to Bill's checking account. Now both Jennifer and Bill could write checks. Bill's name was added to Jennifer's savings account. Both Bill and Jennifer could deposit money and make withdrawals.

But there was less than $300 in the checking account. And there was only $5 in the savings account! They had left $5 in savings just to keep the account open. They had spent the rest of the money on their wedding trip and on things for their apartment.

Jennifer said they had learned the first "law" of consumer education: *Everything costs more than you think it's going to cost.*

Jennifer wanted to start a budget, but Bill put it off. He said, "We'll start a budget one of these days." Bill did not worry about money. After all, they were earning a lot more now than they had been before they got married. Bill thought it would be easy to make ends meet.

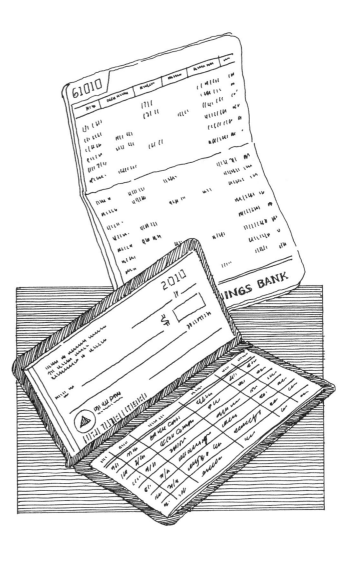

In Chapter 1, Bill and Jennifer made an estimate. They tried to guess how much money they would need. Now let's find out how much their *real* earnings are when they are both working full time.

1. Jennifer earns $7.50 an hour. She works 40 hours a week. She is paid once every two weeks. How much is her base pay? _____

These four taxes are taken out of each paycheck:

$90.00	federal income tax
6.00	state income tax
45.00	Social Security tax
7.20	disability tax

2. How much is taken out of each paycheck in taxes? _____

3. How much is Jennifer's take-home pay? _____

4. Bill earns $7.00 an hour. He works 40 hours a week. Bill also is paid once every two weeks. How much is his base pay? _____

These four taxes are taken out of each paycheck:

$84.00	federal income tax
5.60	state income tax
42.06	Social Security tax
6.72	disability tax

5. How much is taken out of Bill's paycheck in taxes? _____

6. How much is Bill's take-home pay? _____

7. How much do Bill and Jennifer earn together in take-home pay every two weeks? _____

8. How much do they earn per year in take-home pay? _____

9. How much is their take-home pay per month? (Divide their yearly take-home pay by 12 months.) _____

One day a small red car was parked outside the warehouse where Bill worked. A sign on the car said, FOR SALE. Bill knew that car! It belonged to Ed Thomas, who worked in the warehouse. Bill knew that Ed took good care of his car. It looked like new!

Bill found Ed and asked him, "Why do you want to sell your car?"

"We need a bigger car," Ed said. "Our kids are getting bigger. They need more room in the back seat."

"Why don't you trade this car in on a new one?" Bill asked.

"I can get more money by selling it myself," Ed answered. Ed wanted $4,800 for the car.

During his lunch break, Bill drove the red car. He wanted to buy it. But he remembered that there was only $5 in the savings account. Bill knew that most people have to borrow money to buy cars. Later, he stopped at National Savings and Loan and talked to Mrs. Franklin. He asked her if he could borrow $4,800.

Bill learned that he and Jennifer could not borrow money. They did not have **credit.** Mrs. Franklin told Bill how to get credit:

"Pick a department store that you like. Open a **charge account** in that store. Charge a few items each month. But pay the bill *in full* as soon as you get it. Then you'll have credit. You can use the store's name as a **credit reference.**"

At home Bill told Jennifer what he had learned. But Jennifer was afraid of charge accounts! "Too many people get into trouble," she said. "They charge too many items. Then they can't pay their charge account bills, and they have to pay interest on them. I've heard that the interest is 18%."

"Yes, I know," Bill said, "but *any* family might need credit sooner or later. That's

Words to Know	About Credit

credit: an agreement that lets a person borrow money to buy something. The person pays the money back later.

charge account: a plan that lets you buy now and pay later.

credit reference: the name of a bank or store where you have a charge account and good credit. Their name can help you when you need to borrow money.

credit card: a plastic card with your name and charge account number on it. It is used to charge things to your account.

why we should start building a good credit record."

Here are some rules that Bill and Jennifer learned about charge accounts:

- You can use a charge account to build a good credit record.
- Use your **credit card** carefully.
- Do not run up any bills that you can't pay *in full* in one month.

FRANKLIN'S

4000 123 456 788

LEE SMITH

Truth in Lending

Periodic Rate (Monthly)	Corresponding Portion of Average Adjusted Daily Balance	Nominal ANNUAL PERCENTAGE RATE
1.5%	of that portion up to and including $1,500	18%
1%	of that portion over $1,500	12%

Consumer Tip

Credit costs money!

A U.S. law says that companies must tell you how much you are paying for credit. Here is the "Truth-in-Lending" statement for a department store credit card.

Remember Jim Jinx from Chapter 1 —who never pays his bills on time? Jim bought a jacket on sale for $31.94 in November. He used a department store charge account.

Here are his bills for November, December, and January. Jim did not pay the $10 minimum charge. In fact, he didn't pay anything at all!

1. Look at the new balance for January. How much did credit cost Jim in two months? _____

DATE	REFERENCE NUMBER	DEPT.	ITEM DESCRIPTION	PURCHASES	PAYMENTS & CREDITS
Nov 05	311	21441	502 Mens Outerwear	31.94	

BILLING CYCLE CLOSING DATE		ACCOUNT NUMBER			PAYMENT SHOULD BE RECEIVED BY BILLING CYCLE CLOSING DATE**
Nov 17 96		1 546 000 668 9		C	Dec 17 96

TYPE OF ACCOUNT	TO YOUR PREVIOUS BALANCE	WE HAVE ADDED FINANCE CHARGE	PURCHASES	DEDUCTED PAYMENTS & CREDITS	YOUR NEW BALANCE IS	MINIMUM PAYMENT NOW DUE
EE	.00	.00	31.94	.00	31.94	10.00

BILLING CYCLE CLOSING DATE	ACCOUNT NUMBER		PAYMENT SHOULD BE RECEIVED BY BILLING CYCLE CLOSING DATE**
Dec 17 96	1 546 000 668 9	A	Jan 17 97

TYPE OF ACCOUNT	TO YOUR PREVIOUS BALANCE	FINANCE CHARGE	PURCHASES	DEDUCTED PAYMENTS & CREDITS	YOUR NEW BALANCE IS	MINIMUM PAYMENT NOW DUE
EE	31.94	.48	.00	.00	32.42	20.00

BILLING CYCLE CLOSING DATE	ACCOUNT NUMBER		PAYMENT SHOULD BE RECEIVED BY BILLING CYCLE CLOSING DATE**
Jan 17 97	1 546 000 668 9	R3	Feb 17 97

TYPE OF ACCOUNT	TO YOUR PREVIOUS BALANCE	FINANCE CHARGE	PURCHASES	DEDUCTED PAYMENTS & CREDITS	YOUR NEW BALANCE IS	MINIMUM PAYMENT NOW DUE
EE	32.42	.49	.00	.00	32.91	30.00

Bill told Ed Thomas, "We can't buy your car. We don't have any cash. And we don't have any credit."

"Why don't you join the **credit union?**" Ed asked.

A credit union is a group of people who join together to give themselves low-cost banking services. Often the members all work for the same company. Bill knew that his company had a credit union. But he didn't know much about it.

"How can the credit union help me?" Bill asked.

Ed explained. "First, you open a savings account with the credit union. You can save up the **down payment** for a car. The credit union pays 4% interest. Then, when you're ready to buy the car, the credit union lends you money."

> ### Money Words
>
> **credit union:** a group of people who pool their savings so they can borrow money at low interest rates.
>
> **down payment:** the amount of money that pays the first part of a bill.

"I think Jennifer would like the credit union," said Bill.

Sometimes it seems that there are two kinds of people: people who like to save and people who like to *spend.* Jim and Jenny Jinx are "spenders." Jennifer is a "saver." Bill was not yet sure which group he belonged to. He knew that he and Jennifer would not always agree about money. They would have to learn to meet each other halfway. Bill made this plan:

"I'll help Jennifer to set up a budget— like she wants me to. The budget would help us to save money in the credit union. If we have savings, Jennifer won't worry about bills and debts. Maybe she'll be willing to open a charge account."

When Jennifer heard this plan, she said OK. She opened a charge account in a department store. Bill joined the credit union and opened a savings account. He had $75 taken out of each paycheck and deposited with the credit union. Bill and Jennifer agreed that they would use this money as a down payment on a car.

Then they both began to work on their budget. Every day they wrote down the amounts they spent. At the end of the month they added up the totals and recorded them on charts.

One day in October, Jennifer left work early because she didn't feel well. The next day she felt worse. So she went to see the family doctor. The doctor said she'd be fine in a few days if she took the medicine he told her to buy. Jennifer's visit to the doctor cost $50. The medicine cost $20.

In November Jennifer went to see the family dentist. She had her teeth cleaned, but she didn't need any fillings. The dentist's bill was $75. That month Bill spent $17.84 for health care items from the drugstore.

In December Bill found out that he needed new contacts. The eye test cost him $60. The contact lenses cost $155.

Jennifer and Bill wrote these costs on their health care chart.

Health Care				
Doctor	**Dentist**	**Hospital**	**Insurance**	**Medicine**
Oct. $50.00				$20.00
Nov.	$75.00			$17.84
Dec. $60.00				$155.00 (contacts)

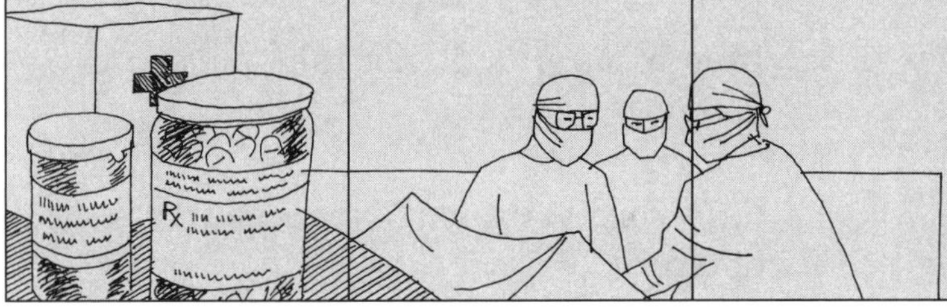

Find how much Jennifer and Bill spent for health care.

1. In October. _____

2. In November. _____

3. In December. _____

4. How much was their average monthly cost for health care? _____

Most people feel that income and spending are personal. So share this activity with your family—not with your class.

A GOOD BUDGET

- helps your family to pay for more of the things you need and want.
- helps every member of the family.

BUDGET PLAN A   If you have a home of your own . . .

1. Each member of the family should have a small notebook.

2. For several months, keep track of all living costs in your notebooks.

3. At the end of each month, add up your costs and write down the totals on these charts.

4. After several months, average the amount you've spent per month on each chart. Use these averages as your first budget.

5. Do not spend more than your budget.

6. Think about ways you could save money for more of the things you need and want.

7. Change the budget as often as you need to. Keep making it better until everyone is happy about the way it works.

BUDGET PLAN B   If you are living with your parents . . .

1. Tell your parents you want to learn how to run a home and how to manage money. Tell them that you need their help.

2. Show your parents this activity. Ask if they would like to share it with you. Explain that they would need to carry notebooks and keep track of their spending. If they agree, see that each family member has a small notebook and gets off to a good start. Be sure to keep your *own* notebook up to date.

3. Now follow the rules under Budget Plan A.

   If your parents do not take part in this activity:

   a. Record your own expenses in a notebook.

   b. At the end of each month, add up the amounts on the charts.

   c. Think about ways you could save money for more of the things you need and want.

Use these charts to write down how
much your family has spent on these items.

Housing			
House payment or rent	Repairs	Insurance	Property tax

Utilities				
Gas	Electricity	Water	Garbage and recycle pickup	Telephone

Food	
Food served at home	**Meals in restaurants**

Transportation					
Car payments	**Gas and oil**	**Insurance/ licenses**	**Repairs**	**Parking/ tolls**	**Cab, bus, trains plane fare**

Household and Personal Needs				
Laundry/ dry cleaning	Cosmetics/ personal care	Haircuts/ beauty shop	Stamps and stationery	Small items for the house

Health Care*				
Doctor	Dentist	Hospital	Insurance	Medicine

*Write down only the costs that come out of your take-home pay. Do not record any costs that your insurance company pays. Do not record health insurance premiums that come out of your paycheck.

Clothing			
Clothes	Shoes	Repairs	Sewing/Cleaning

Savings	
Short-term	Investment

Recreation					
Games and shows	Crafts/hobbies	Club dues	Pets	Vacations/trips	Other

Big Items for the Home		
Purchases	Payments	Repairs

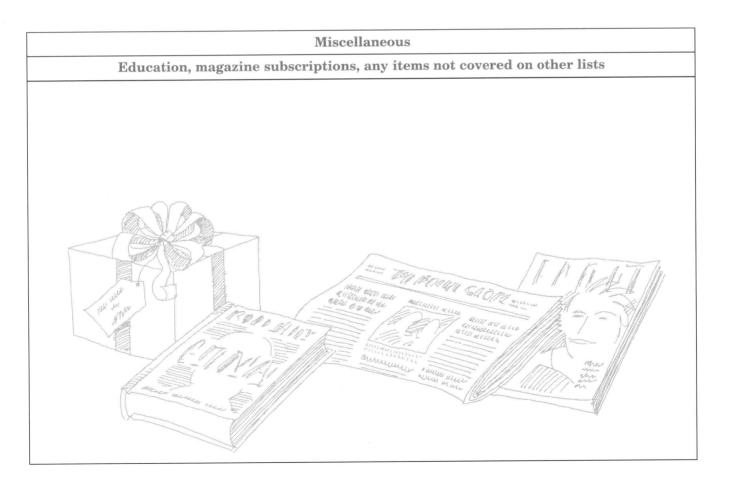

Miscellaneous
Education, magazine subscriptions, any items not covered on other lists

1. There are two kinds of expenses in the family budget. *Fixed* expenses are costs that stay the same every month. Rent is a fixed expense. *Flexible* expenses are costs that change from month to month. Utility bills are flexible, for example, because you use more light and heat in the winter. Name some other fixed and flexible expenses. (Check the headings on the budget chart for ideas.) If you had to cut your spending, what kind of expenses could you cut?

2. People get into debt by spending more than they earn. Suppose you found this happening to you. Which items in the budget would be easy to cut? Would you move into a cheaper house or apartment? Would you sell your car and ride the bus? Or would you look for a better job and hope to earn more money?

3. Some families put cash in budget envelopes each month. Each envelope is marked—"clothing," "recreation," and so on. Suppose there is $35 in the recreation envelope. When the $35 is used up, the family must stop spending money on recreation. Is it a good idea to put money in envelopes to keep track of spending? Why or why not?

4. Most families pay their bills by check. If you pay by check, how would you keep track of the amount spent on each item in the budget?

TEST YOURSELF

Today you can buy almost *anything* in a food store. But in this book, the food budget covers only one thing: family nutrition. (*Nutrition* is food that leads to growth and good health.)

Below is a list of items you could buy in a supermarket. Make a check on the chart to show where each item belongs in the family budget. (Review Chapter 1 if you need help.)

	Food	Transportation	Personal and Household Needs	Health Care	Clothing	Recreation
1. cheese						
2. toothbrush						
3. bananas						
4. bread						
5. socks						
6. aspirin						
7. paring knife						
8. milk						
9. magazine						
10. rice						
11. motor oil						
12. ground beef						
13. kite						
14. detergent						
15. picnic cooler						

ANSWERS:

1. food 2. personal needs 3. food 4. food 5. clothing 6. health care 7. household needs 8. food 9. recreation 10. food 11. transportation 12. food 13. recreation 14. household needs 15. recreation

Here are the amounts that Sue Takata spent on clothes in five months.

Clothing			
Clothes	**Shoes**	**Repairs**	**Sewing/Cleaning**
Mar. $19.65 $63.40			$15.66
Apr. $57.51			$17.86
May $25.00	$51.30		$6.39
June $21.05	$51.30	$13.85	$14.91
July $40.65 $32.95	$43.81		

How much is the monthly average? _____

ANSWER:

$95.06

Comparison Shopping

Preview: Shopping for the Best Buy

Two stores are having sales on stainless steel cookware. Store B is selling seven pieces (four pots and three lids) for $49.99.

How much would these same seven pieces cost on sale at Store A?

1. $1\frac{1}{2}$-quart saucepan _____

2. 2-quart saucepan _____

3. $4\frac{1}{2}$-quart dutch oven _____

4. 9-inch skillet _____

5. Total _____

How much would the same seven pieces cost at regular price at Store A?

6. $1\frac{1}{2}$-quart saucepan _____

7. 2-quart saucepan _____

8. $4\frac{1}{2}$-quart dutch oven _____

9. 9-inch skillet _____

10. Total _____

11. Which store is offering you the "best buy"? _____

12. How much can you save (off regular price) by buying the seven-piece set at Store B? _____

Store A

SAVE UP TO 50%
COOK WITH CONFIDENCE

Shiny stainless steel cookware has the plus of copper-clad bottoms for even heat distribution. Pick the pieces you like best and savor the savings!

covered saucepans:
$1\frac{1}{2}$ quart, reg. $17.00 .... $12.00
2 quart, reg. $19.00 .... $14.00
$4\frac{1}{2}$ quart oven, reg. $27.00 .... $17.00
9" open skillet, reg. $19.50 .... $9.75

Store B

7-PIECE COOKWARE SETS

Stainless steel cookware with copper bottom set includes $1\frac{1}{2}$ and 2-Qt. covered saucepans, $4\frac{1}{2}$-Qt. Dutch oven and 9-in. open skillet.

If Each Piece Purchased Separately
$82.50

7-PIECE SET $49.99

Comparison Shopping

Bill and Jennifer have set a **goal.** They want to buy a car. They are saving $200 a month to reach this goal.

Nina and Jose have a goal, too. They want to have a baby. They plan to save money for a year. Then they can afford to have a child.

Ed and Anne Thomas want to buy a home of their own. Their goal is a house with a yard for the children to play in.

What happens when people set goals? They feel they have something to work for. They know where they are going. They are willing to save or spend money in ways that help them carry out their plan.

So Jennifer and Bill have begun to save and to keep track of their spending. They look for ways to buy the things they need without spending so much money.

One day Jose stopped at their door. "Nina and I are going to the **flea market,**" he said. "Would you like to go along?"

"That's a good idea," Jennifer said. "We can buy pans for our kitchen. Pans should be cheap at the flea market."

At the big open-air market they saw all kinds of items on tables and in open sheds. You could buy almost anything at the flea market! Some items were new, but others were **secondhand.**

Some of the old pots and pans were still dirty from use. Jennifer and Bill did not stop to look at those. But at last they found secondhand pans that were clean and looked like new. They also found some brand-new pans that seemed to be priced very low.

At the flea market, Jennifer and Bill bought these secondhand items:

10-cup automatic drip coffee maker	$25.00
$2\frac{1}{2}$-quart stainless steel tea kettle	5.00
10-inch iron skillet	9.00
8-inch iron skillet	7.00

$2\frac{1}{2}$ QT. TEA KETTLE

REG. $18.00
NOW **$15.00**

Later, they found some beautiful red cookware. These pots and pans were new. They could buy five pans for $69.95.

A newspaper ad was taped to the table beside the red pans. The ad said the same set cost $99.95 in a department store. Jennifer and Bill bought the whole set. They were happy to save $30!

They found a box of five knives on sale for $8. The knives were new and looked very pretty in the box. Jennifer and Bill bought the knives also.

Then they had to go home. They could not carry any more bags or boxes!

1. How much did they spend at the flea market? _____

Later, Bill showed Jennifer an ad in the newspaper. The ad showed a stainless steel tea kettle on sale for $15. "Look at this!" he said. "We saved $10 on our tea kettle."

Then they began to look at other ads in the paper.

At the flea market, Jennifer and Bill had spent $18 for two iron skillets. At a discount store, they could have bought two iron skillets for only $14.92!

Bill and Jennifer had spent $69.95 for five red pots and pans. At the department store they could have bought five stainless steel pans for $65.

CAST IRON COOKWARE
- 1-Qt. Covered Sauce Pan
- 2-Qt. Covered Sauce Pan
- $4\frac{1}{2}$-Qt. Dutch Oven Cover
- $6\frac{1}{2}$" Open Skillet
- 8" Open Skillet
- $10\frac{1}{2}$" Open Skillet

SPECIAL 2–10" SKILLETS $14.92

Reg. $65.95 **$58.44**

STAINLESS STEEL COOKWARE

A fine tradition and a great buy. Good cooks like you know the best menu always begins with the finest cookware. Now, find a terrific price on your choice of copper or stainless bottoms that spread heat evenly. The 8-pc. set: $1\frac{1}{2}$, 2-qt. cov. saucepans, 6-qt. cov. stock pot, the 7", 9" open skillets are basic. Lids are all interchangeable to fit skillets. Housewares.

6-PC SET; OPEN STOCK VALUE, $88.50 **$65.00**

Jennifer and Bill had paid $8 for a set of five knives. A discount store was selling a 17-piece set for $5.88. But at a department store, one French chef's knife was on sale for $24.50.

"Did we pay too much for the knives?" Jennifer asked. "Or did we pay too little?"

"Maybe the knives we bought are too cheap," Bill answered. "If so, they won't stay sharp very long."

"Yes," said Jennifer. "We have to think about quality as well as price. A knife that is good quality will last a long time."

"But it's hard to tell good quality in an ad!" said Bill. "We should go to the store and look at them."

2. How much would Jennifer and Bill pay for these five knives at the department store sale price?

paring knife _____

butcher knife _____

French chef's knife _____

roast slicer _____

bread slicer _____

Total _____

Less 20% _____

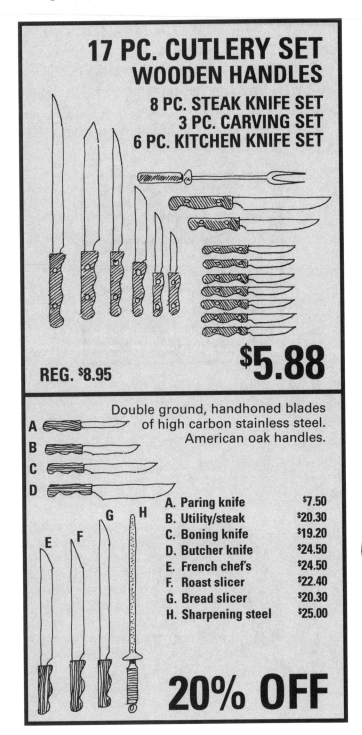

17 PC. CUTLERY SET
WOODEN HANDLES

8 PC. STEAK KNIFE SET
3 PC. CARVING SET
6 PC. KITCHEN KNIFE SET

$5.88

REG. $8.95

Double ground, handhoned blades of high carbon stainless steel. American oak handles.

A.
B.
C.
D.
E. F. G. H.

A. Paring knife	$7.50
B. Utility/steak	$20.30
C. Boning knife	$19.20
D. Butcher knife	$24.50
E. French chef's	$24.50
F. Roast slicer	$22.40
G. Bread slicer	$20.30
H. Sharpening steel	$25.00

20% OFF

Consumer Tip

Jennifer and Bill had taken the first steps in comparison shopping:

Step 1—Price   Of course, you want to pay a low price. You compare prices to see which store has the lowest price for the item you want to buy.

Step 2—Quality   You don't always have to buy the very best. But you want to buy good things that will last a long time.

Comparison shopping means comparing price, comparing quality, and then buying from the store that gives you the best quality at the lowest cost.

Jennifer and Bill walked to the shopping center to look at kitchen items. At a discount store they found iron skillets, coffee pots, and tea kettles like the ones they had bought at the flea market. They compared the prices:

Item	Flea Market	Discount Store
10-cup coffee maker	25.00	19.95
$2\frac{1}{2}$-quart stainless steel tea kettle	5.00	12.95
10-inch iron skillet	9.00	7.46
8-inch iron skillet	7.00	6.39

3. How much did they spend on these four items at the flea market? _____

4. How much would the same four items cost at the discount store? _____

5. How much could Bill and Jennifer save by buying just the iron skillets at the discount store? _____

At a department store, Jennifer and Bill found some red pans. These pans were almost the same as the ones they had bought at the flea market. They were made by the same company.

They talked to the sales clerk about the red pans. "We have some pans almost like these," Jennifer said. "But ours are not as heavy."

The clerk explained: "You bought the lightweight set. The company doesn't make that set any more. We used to sell the set for $89.95."

So Jennifer and Bill had really saved $20 by buying the red pans at the flea market.

Here are the prices of the new, heavy pans.

SALE
TOP QUALITY COOKWARE

2 qt. saucepan $28.99
3 qt. saucepan $40.99
4 qt. sauce pot $46.99
8 qt. sauce pot $50.00
$10\frac{1}{2}$" open fry pan $20.99

6. How much would these five pans cost all together? _____

Consumer Tip

Save time and gas or bus fare. Use your phone for comparison shopping.

Suppose you see something you like in a store, but you think the price is too high. Write down some notes about:
- the name of the item
- the name of the company that makes it
- the model number (if the company makes more than one model)
- the color or size you want—or anything else that's important to you

Then call other stores on the phone. Ask how much this item costs in the other stores.

"We made some mistakes at the flea market," Jennifer said.

"Yes," said Bill. "We thought that things are always cheaper at the flea market. That isn't true."

"We should have bought two good knives," Jennifer said. "We need a paring knife and a slicing knife. And two good knives would be more useful than five cheap ones."

"And we paid too much for the iron skillets," Bill added. "Iron skillets are cheaper at the discount store."

"Now we have four skillets—two iron ones and two red ones," Jennifer said. "Do we really need four skillets?"

"We should have made a shopping list," said Bill. "Next time we go to the flea market, let's make a list of the things we really need."

"Good idea!" said Jennifer. "But let's check the prices at the discount store *before* we go to the flea market!"

"OK," said Bill. "And let's check the prices at the department store, too. Then we'll know a good buy if we see one at the flea market. We could check out some garage sales, too."

"I'm glad we bought the red pans at the flea market," said Jennifer.

"So am I," Bill answered. "Maybe our trip to the flea market wasn't so bad after all."

Five small appliances are on sale in this ad. All five are made by well-known companies. You can find these items (or items almost like them) in your own city.

Find out how much you would have to pay for these appliances. Check at least one department store and one discount store. Check any other store that you choose. Write the prices on this chart.

	DEPARTMENT STORE	DISCOUNT STORE	ANY OTHER STORE
SPECIAL 2 SLICE PASTRY TOASTER HEAT SETTING SELECTOR $15	Name of store: Price:	Name of store: Price:	Name of store: Price:
SALE STEAM & DRY IRON WITH 25 VENTS WATER WINDOW & SELECTOR REG. $19.99 $14	Name of store: Price:	Name of store: Price:	Name of store: Price:

	DEPARTMENT STORE	DISCOUNT STORE	ANY OTHER STORE
SPECIAL **3-SPEED HAND MIXER** **$12**	Name of store: Price:	Name of store: Price:	Name of store: Price:
SALE **ELECTRIC CAN OPENER** REG. $16.99 **$15**	Name of store: Price:	Name of store: Price:	Name of store: Price:
SPECIAL **PUSH-BUTTON PHONE** **$27**	Name of store: Price:	Name of store: Price:	Name of store: Price:

White Sale! White Sale! Sheets and towels were on sale in all the stores. Jennifer and Bill saw the ads in the Sunday paper. The ads gave the regular price and the sale price for each item.

At a department store, bath towels were on sale for $18 each. The ad said the regular price was $25 for each towel.

At a discount store, bath towels were on sale at two for $7. The regular price was $5.44 each.

On Monday Jennifer went to the discount store to see the towels advertised at two for $7. They were almost as thin as dish towels! Jennifer thought, "These towels would wear out in a few months."

Next she stopped at the department store and looked at the towels on sale for $18 each. They were almost as thick as rugs! "But $18 is too much for one towel," Jennifer decided.

Then she saw a lot of bath towels piled on a table. The sign said, "2 for $15—$9.99 each if perfect." These were good, thick towels, but each towel had something wrong with it. Sometimes it was just a snag—a place where one thread had pulled out. It was hard to find the flaws in the towels. Jennifer thought these towels were the best buy. She bought six bath towels and six washcloths.

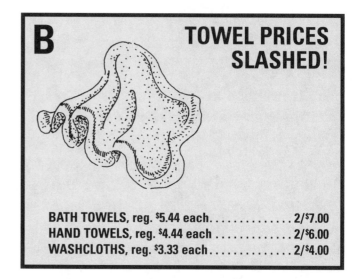

B TOWEL PRICES SLASHED!

BATH TOWELS, reg. $5.44 each . . . . 2/$7.00
HAND TOWELS, reg. $4.44 each . . . . 2/$6.00
WASHCLOTHS, reg. $3.33 each . . . . 2/$4.00

C FLUFFY BATH TOWELS

SPECIAL PURCHASE
BATH TOWELS (if perfect $9.99 each) 2 for $15
WASHCLOTHS (if perfect $4.75 each) 2 for $2.25

Colorful bath towels—yours at these low, low prices. Choose from a wide assortment of prints. All woven in soft and absorbent cotton/ polyester terry. And, the minor imperfections won't affect wear or appearance.

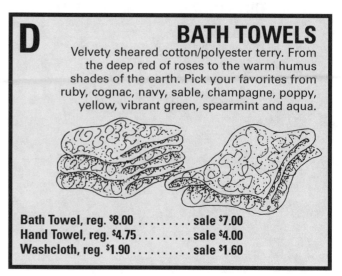

D BATH TOWELS
Velvety sheared cotton/polyester terry. From the deep red of roses to the warm humus shades of the earth. Pick your favorites from ruby, cognac, navy, sable, champagne, poppy, yellow, vibrant green, spearmint and aqua.

Bath Towel, reg. $8.00 . . . . sale $7.00
Hand Towel, reg. $4.75 . . . . sale $4.00
Washcloth, reg. $1.90 . . . . sale $1.60

A PLUSH COTTON TERRY TOWELS
In white, navy, vanilla, bordeaux, teal, lemon, and brown

Bath Towel, reg. $25.00 . . . . $18.00
Hand Towel, reg. $15.00 . . . . $10.00
Washcloth, reg. $8.00 . . . . $6.00

1. Look at Ad C. Jennifer bought six bath towels and six washcloths at the sale price.

   a. How much did she pay for the bath towels? _____

   b. How much did she pay for the washcloths? _____

   c. How much did Jennifer spend on the bath towels and washcloths? _____

   Now find out how much these same items would cost at the regular price if perfect.

   d. Six bath towels _____

   e. Six washcloths _____

   f. Total _____

   g. How much did Jennifer save? _____

2. Look at Ad D. Find the cost of two bath towels, two hand towels, and two washcloths at the sale price.

   a. Two bath towels _____

   b. Two hand towels _____

   c. Two washcloths _____

   d. Total _____

3. Find the cost of five bath towels at the sale price in each ad.

   a. Ad A _____

   b. Ad B _____

   c. Ad C _____

   d. Ad D _____

   e. Ad E _____

   f. Ad F _____

E

COLORFUL TOWEL ENSEMBLES

Velvety soft sheared terry towels add new drama to your bath decor in vibrant solid colors. Thirsty cotton/polyester; hemmed ends.

Hand Towel, reg. $3.99		$3.59
Washcloth, reg. $2.49		$2.19
Fingertip Towel, reg. $2.49		$2.29

BATH TOWEL REGULAR $4.99   **$3.99**

F

Bath towels of thick, absorbent 100% cotton. In radiant solids plus floral and striped jacquards.

BATH SIZE REGULAR $6.99   **$5.99**

Good consumers plan ahead. They make shopping lists. They buy things they really need. They compare prices and buy wisely.

But most shoppers waste money by buying on impulse. The shopper sees something nice in a store—something like a camera. The shopper says, "Maybe it would be fun to have a camera! I'll buy it!" "Buying on impulse" means buying something you don't really need and had not planned to buy.

Jennifer saw an ad for a camera in the paper. "Look, Bill," she said. "We could save $14 by buying this camera on sale."

"Don't buy it now," Bill said. "I'll give it to you for your birthday."

Jennifer tried to smile. But she didn't feel very happy. Her birthday was four months away!

A month later, Jennifer saw another ad. The same camera was now on sale for $78.99. "Maybe we should buy the camera now," Jennifer said. But Bill only laughed.

Bill had seen the same camera at a discount store. The discount store's regular price was only $75.88.

Bill watched the ads for a few more weeks. Then the discount store had a sale. Now the camera was marked down to $69.99. Bill bought the camera. He gave it to Jennifer for her birthday.

"Watch the ads for several months," Bill said, "when you want to buy something you don't need right away."

1. Jennifer wanted to buy a camera for $78.99. Bill bought the same camera for only $69.99. How much did he save by waiting for a good price? _____

2. When Bill bought the camera, he spent $9.99 for a case to put it in. How much did he spend for both items? _____

3. Jennifer can save money by watching the ads and buying film on sale.

   A camera store sells a roll of film for $4.80. How much will Jennifer save on each roll if she buys her film on sale at $3.12? _____

4. Jennifer gets 24 pictures from each roll of film. How much does each picture cost at $4.80 a roll? _____

5. How much does each picture cost at $3.12 a roll? _____

AUTO-FOCUS POCKET CAMERA
No more out-of-focus pictures. Auto-load and rewind.

ONLY $78.99

AUTO-FOCUS POCKET CAMERA
SALE $69.99
REG. $75.88
Clear, crisp pictures at the push of a button. Fully automated.

VINYL CASE
$9.99

35 mm FILM
24 EXPOSURE
NOW
$3.12

Answer these questions *yes* or *no*. Then talk about your answers with the class.

1. A new refrigerator works just fine—but it has a big dent in its door. And you do not know how to fix it. The store would sell the refrigerator at $50 off the regular price.
Would you buy this refrigerator?

Choose from washers, dryers and refrigerators, all slightly damaged or dented.
This is a great way to buy what you need at a special price. All in working condition. Pick the color you want.

SAVE

Choose from bedroom, dining room, living room, family room, and dinette furniture, slightly damaged or dented. Over 200 items to choose from! Find something just right for you.

SAVE

2. A washing machine has been marked down $250—but it doesn't work! The salesperson says, "We don't do repairs here at the store. But I'll give you the name of a shop that can fix it."
Would you buy this washer?

3. A chest of drawers is marked down 50%. The chest is in good shape. But some handles are missing from the drawers. Would you buy this chest?

4. One arm of a chair is broken. But you know how to fix it. You could make it look as good as new. The chair is marked down 30%.
Would you buy this chair?

5. There is a big scratch on the top of a bookcase. But you could paint the bookcase to match your walls. The bookcase is marked 20% off.
Would you buy this bookcase?

6. Do you ever see garage sales near your home or school? If so, try this activity: Find out what you could buy for $3 at a garage sale.
a. Each person in your class should go to one garage sale.
b. At the garage sale, pick out some things you like. Find out the prices of these items. Make a list of items you could buy for $3 or less.
c. Pick a good item that costs more than $3. Ask the owner, "Would you sell it to me for $3?" If the answer is yes, add that item to your list.
d. Read your list of $3 items to the class.

NAME _____

Here are ten sale items—two of each kind. Each ad gives the regular price and the sale price. Find the sale price for each item. Then check the one that costs the least.

1.

A
Reg. Price $279
SALE:
50% OFF

B
Reg. Price $249
SALE:
10% OFF

2.

C
Reg. Price $349.98
SALE:
20% OFF

D
Reg. Price $295.88
SALE:
Marked
down $50

3.

E
Reg. Price $289.95
SALE:
Marked
down $85

F
Reg. Price
$129.95
SALE:
20% OFF

4.

G
Reg. Price $149.99
SALE: 75% OFF

H
Reg. Price $99.98
SALE: 20% OFF

5.

I
Reg. Price $39.95
SALE:
20% OFF

J
Reg. Price $39.95
SALE:
Marked down $8.50

1. Which chair costs the least?   A _____   B _____

2. Which TV set costs the least?   C _____   D _____

3. Which camera costs the least?   E _____   F _____

4. Which tent costs the least?   G _____   H _____

5. Which radio costs the least?   I _____   J _____

ANSWERS:

1.A 2.D 3.F 4.G 5.J

Read each of these sentences. Then put an X under *true* or *false*.

True	False	
_____	_____	**1.** Everything always costs less at a flea market.
_____	_____	**2.** You can do comparison shopping by phone.
_____	_____	**3.** Low-cost items are never good quality.
_____	_____	**4.** Comparison shopping means comparing prices, comparing quality, and then buying from the store that gives you the best quality at the lowest cost.
_____	_____	**5.** You should watch the ads for several months when you want to buy something that you don't need right away.
_____	_____	**6.** Impulse buying helps people to save money.
_____	_____	**7.** Setting goals makes people feel they have something to work for.
_____	_____	**8.** Making a shopping list is just a waste of time.
_____	_____	**9.** Some secondhand items are as good as new.
_____	_____	**10.** A broken chair is never a good buy at any price.

ANSWERS:

1. F 2. T 3. F 4. T 5. T 6. F 7. T 8. F 9. T 10. F

NAME _____

Shopping for Food

Preview: Comparing Prices

Suppose you have been buying meat at Store A. Now a friend tells you that meat costs less at Store B.

You have these three items on your shopping list:

2 lbs. butterfish fillets
3 lbs. fryer legs
5 lbs. London broil

Find out how much these three items would cost at each store. Use the prices in the ads on this page.

Store A
1. 2 lbs. butterfish _____
2. 3 lbs. fryer legs _____
3. 5 lbs. London broil _____
4. Total _____

Store B
5. 2 lbs. butterfish _____
6. 3 lbs. fryer legs _____
7. 5 lbs. London broil _____
8. Total _____
9. Could you save money by shopping at Store B? _____

Store A

FRESH **GROUND BEEF**
FRESH GROUND IN OUR STORES DAILY.
FAT CONTENT LESS THAN 30%.
LB. **$1.39**

BEEF ROUND **LONDON BROIL**
USDA CHOICE GRADE, THICK, JUICY
CUTS OF TOP ROUND and SIRLOIN TIP.
LB. **$2.99**

FRYER LEGS
WHOLE LEGS
LB. **$.69**

FRESH FILLET OF
BUTTERFISH
LB. **$3.19**

Store B

USDA WHOLE
FRESH FRYER LEGS
PER LB. **$.79**

BEEF TOP ROUND
LONDON BROIL
PER LB. **$3.19**

FROZEN 1 LB. PKG. COOKED
MEATBALLS
EACH. **$1.79**

WATER ADDED WHOLE OR HALF
BONELESS HAM
PER LB. **$1.89**

BLACKCOD
BUTTERFISH FILLETS
PER LB. **$2.99**

ANSWERS:

1. $6.38 2. $2.07 3. $14.95 4. $23.40 5. $5.98 6. $2.37 7. $15.95 8. $24.30 9. No.

Shopping for Food

"Our budget looks good on paper," Jennifer said. "But it's not so easy to follow! Last month we spent too much money on food."

"Maybe we went out to dinner too often," said Bill. "Eating in restaurants is a good way to run up the food bill."

"We eat lunch in restaurants, too," Jennifer pointed out. "I guess we really should pack our lunches at home."

"I'd rather have a hot lunch," said Bill. "But you're right. Brown-bag lunches save a lot of money."

"I can think of another mistake we've made," Jennifer said. "We eat too many frozen dinners. We're both tired after work at night. We just don't feel like cooking."

Bill nodded. "Remember those frozen meat pies? They didn't taste very good. And there was hardly any meat in them!"

"There isn't much **nutrition** in meatless meat pies," Jennifer said. "I wish I knew more about buying food. We want to save money—but we want to stay healthy, too. Is it possible to eat *better* for less money?"

"My mother is a good consumer," said Bill. "Maybe she could give us some tips."

Jennifer called Mrs. Rossi and explained the problem. "We want to learn how to buy better food and save money."

Mrs. Rossi said she could come over to Holly House on Thursday evening. "The food store ads are in the paper every Wednesday," she said. "Every Wednesday I make out my weekly shopping list. So Thursday will be a good time to talk about **comparison shopping.**"

Words to Know	About Food

nutrition: food that leads to growth and good health.

comparison shopping: comparing price and quality; buying an item with the best quality at the lowest cost.

Here is the shopping list that Mrs. Rossi showed to Jennifer and Bill on Thursday evening.

Shopping List	
MEATS & FISH	
3 lbs. pork spare ribs	
5 lbs. beef rib roast	
2 lbs. chicken legs	
FRUITS & VEGETABLES	
1 pineapple	
3 lbs. peaches	
1 lb. cherries	
2 lbs. green beans	
2 bunches green onions	
2 bunches radishes	
2 heads lettuce	
GROCERIES	
barbecue sauce	
fruit punch	
snack crackers	
DAIRY-DELICATESSEN	
American cheese	
ODDS & ENDS	
Charcoal	

Each week Mrs. Rossi checked the food store ads. Then she made a list of the items she wanted to buy. She tried to find out which stores had the lowest prices.

There were two food stores in the shopping center near Holly House: the Super Saver Market and the Thrift Mart.

There were 15 items on Mrs. Rossi's list. Jennifer checked the prices of these items in the Super Saver ad. She found out how much all 15 items would cost at the Super Saver Market.

1. How much would these three meat items cost?

3 lbs. pork spareribs   _____

5 lbs. boneless cross rib roast   _____

2 lbs. chicken legs   _____

TOTAL   _____

$uper $aver Market

FRESH DAILY

SUPER SAVER MEATS

LONDON BROIL . . . . . . $2.69 LB.

PORK SPARERIBS . . . $2.39 LB.

SMOKED HAMS . . . . . $1.79 LB.

SIRLOIN TIP ROAST $2.49 LB.

CANNED HAM . . . . . . $8.59 EA.

FRESH FRYERS . . . . . . $1.29 LB.

SUPER SAVER POULTRY

BBQ STEAK
BONELESS BEEF CROSS RIB . . . . . . LB. $2.19

CHUCK STEAK
BONELESS BEEF CENTER CUT . . . . LB. $1.79

CHUCK ROAST
BONELESS BEEF . . . . LB. $1.55

CHUCK ROAST
BONELESS BEEF CENTER . . . . LB. $1.75

RUMP ROAST
BONELESS BEEF ROUND . . . . LB. $1.95

CROSS RIB ROAST
BONELESS BEEF CHUCK . . . . LB. $2.65

BEEF STEW
BONELESS . . . . LB. $1.79

CHICKEN LEGS
MEATY DRUMSTICKS . . . . LB. $1.09

CHICKEN WINGS
GOOD SNACKS . . . . LB. $.69

TURKEYS
8–25 LBS . . . . LB. $.89

2. How much would these seven produce items cost at the Super Saver Market?

1 pineapple _____

3 lbs. peaches _____

1 lb. cherries _____

2 lbs. green beans _____

2 bunches green onions _____

2 bunches radishes _____

2 heads lettuce _____

TOTAL _____

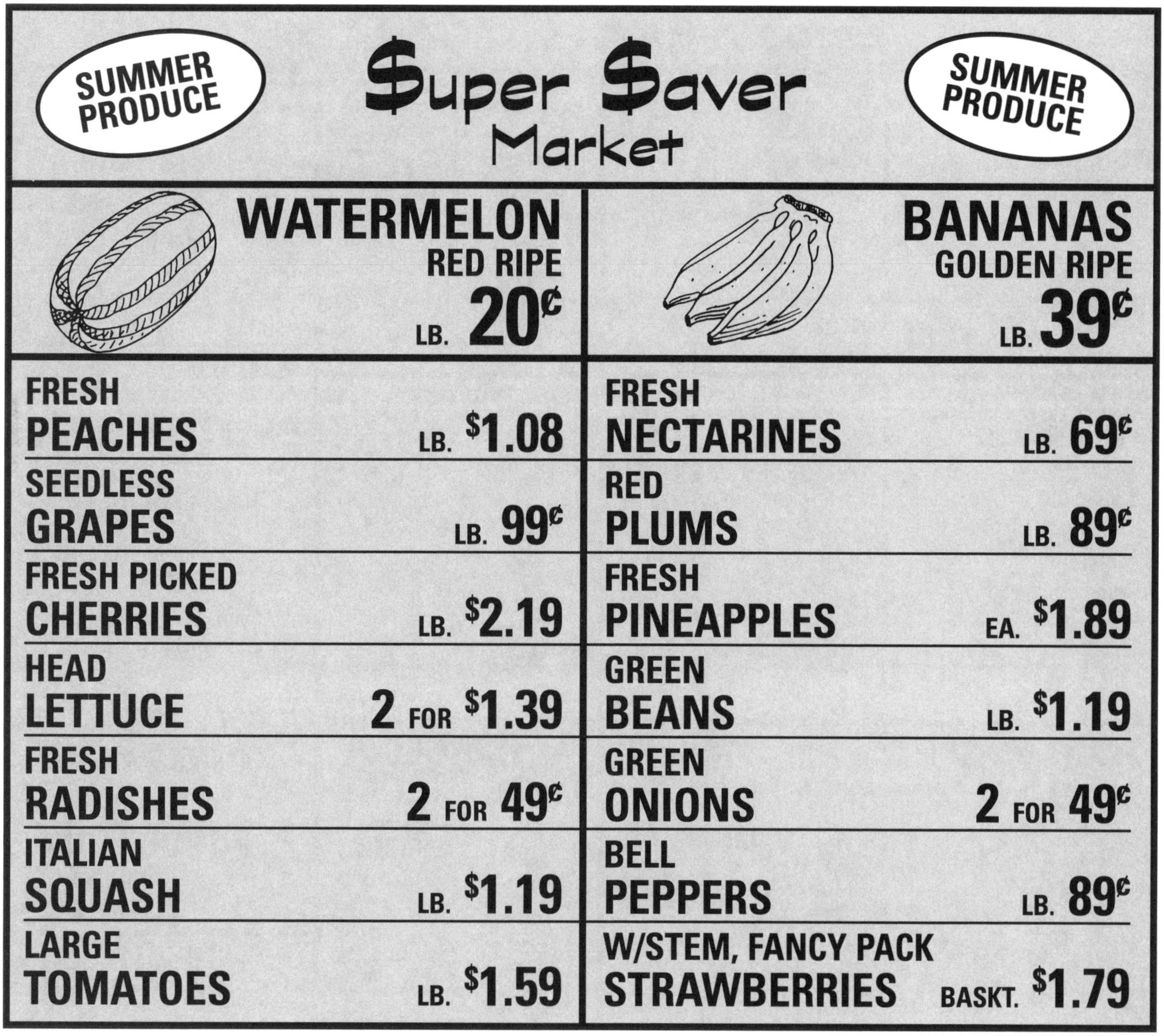

SUMMER PRODUCE	$uper $aver Market		SUMMER PRODUCE
	WATERMELON RED RIPE LB. **20¢**	**BANANAS** GOLDEN RIPE LB. **39¢**	
FRESH **PEACHES** LB. **$1.08**		FRESH **NECTARINES** LB. **69¢**	
SEEDLESS **GRAPES** LB. **99¢**		RED **PLUMS** LB. **89¢**	
FRESH PICKED **CHERRIES** LB. **$2.19**		FRESH **PINEAPPLES** EA. **$1.89**	
HEAD **LETTUCE** 2 FOR **$1.39**		GREEN **BEANS** LB. **$1.19**	
FRESH **RADISHES** 2 FOR **49¢**		GREEN **ONIONS** 2 FOR **49¢**	
ITALIAN **SQUASH** LB. **$1.19**		BELL **PEPPERS** LB. **89¢**	
LARGE **TOMATOES** LB. **$1.59**		W/STEM, FANCY PACK **STRAWBERRIES** BASKT. **$1.79**	

3. How much would these five grocery items cost at the Super Saver Market?

barbecue sauce	_____
fruit punch	_____
snack crackers	_____
American cheese	_____
charcoal briquets	_____
TOTAL	_____

4. What is the total cost of the 15 items at the Super Saver Market?

meat	_____
produce	_____
groceries	_____
TOTAL	_____

$uper $aver Market

CHARCOAL BRIQUETS
10-LB. BAG
$4.89

MARSHMALLOWS
59¢
10-OZ. PKG.

MIXED NUTS
WITH PEANUTS
$2.99
12-OZ. CAN

CHEESES

AMERICAN CHEESE
12-OZ. PKG. **$1.79**

CRACKER SPREAD
8-OZ. **$1.49**

CHEDDAR CHEESE
8-OZ. PKG. **$1.27**

BREAD
FRESH BAKE
CELLO WRAPPED
16-OZ. LOAF **69¢**

BREAD
FRESH BAKE
CELLO WRAPPED
1½-LB. LOAF **$1.09**

MARGARINE
REG. 1 LB. CTN.
85¢

SNACK CRACKERS
ASSORTED VARIETIES
$1.49
PER PKG.

MUSTARD
$1.98
24-OZ. JAR

FRUIT PUNCH
$1.99
12-OZ. CAN

PICKLES
DILL HALVES &
KOSHER STYLE
DILL HALVES
$1.59
22-OZ. JAR

BARBECUE SAUCE
ASSORTED VARIETIES
$2.39
16-OZ. BTL.

MUFFINS
FRESH BAKE ENGLISH
14-OZ. PKG. **99¢**

HOT DOG BUNS
FRESH BAKE
8-PACK **$1.15**

HAMBURGER BUNS
FRESH BAKE
8-PACK **$1.15**

Bill checked the prices of the 15 items in the Thrift Mart ad. He found out how much the 15 items would cost all together at the Thrift Mart.

5. How much would these three meat items cost at the Thrift Mart?

3 lbs. pork spareribs _____

5 lbs. boneless cross rib roast _____

2 lbs. chicken legs _____

TOTAL _____

THRIFT MART
SAVINGS ON QUALITY MEATS

BONELESS USDA CHOICE
CHUCK STEAKS
OR ROASTS .... LB. **$1.49**

FRESH FRYER PARTS
MEATY DRUMSTICKS .... LB. **98¢**
(BREAST & THIGHS: $1.09 LB.)

CROSS RIB OVEN ROAST
BONELESS USDA TENDER BEEF CHUCK .... LB. **$1.89**

BABY SIZE PORK SPARERIBS
LEAN MEATY RIBS. 3 LBS. AND UNDER FRESHLY THAWED .... LB. **$3.09**

LEAN BBQ STEAKS
BONELESS USDA TENDER BEEF CHUCK .... LB. **$2.56**

6. How much would these seven produce items cost at the Thrift Mart?

1 pineapple _____

3 lbs. peaches _____

1 lb. cherries _____

2 lbs. green beans _____

2 bunches green onions _____

2 bunches radishes _____

2 heads lettuce _____

TOTAL _____

THRIFT MART
SUMMER PRODUCE SALE

GREEN ONIONS & RADISHES — 2 FOR **45¢**	**PLUMS SANTA ROSA** — LB. **69¢**
NECTARINES SWEET & RIPE — LB. **59¢**	**PEACHES/TRY PEACHES & CREAM** — LB. **98¢**
NORTHWEST BING CHERRIES — LB. **$2.49**	**HONEYDEW MELONS** — LB. **29¢**
PINEAPPLES/ISLAND TASTE TREAT — EA. **98¢**	**RIPE AVOCADOS** — EA. **39¢**
GREEN BEANS FARM FRESH — LB. **99¢**	**HEAD LETTUCE GARDEN FRESH** — EA. **76¢**

7. How much would these five grocery items cost at the Thrift Mart?

barbecue sauce _____

fruit punch _____

snack crackers _____

American cheese _____

charcoal briquets _____

TOTAL _____

8. How much would the 15 items cost all together at the Thrift Mart?

Meat _____

Produce _____

Groceries _____

TOTAL _____

9. Jennifer and Bill compared the totals they had added up. Which store is cheaper?

_____

BARBECUE SAUCE
PLAIN, HICKORY, HOT 18-OZ. BTL.
REG. $2.19

$1.98

THRIFT MART

SPECIALS

DELI DELIGHTS MONTEREY JACK CHEESE
REG. $2.89 LB.

LB. **$2.40**

PEOPLE PLEASERS

STYROFOAM CUPS 51 CT. PKG. REG. 85¢ .... **79¢**

HOT FUDGE TOPPING 5-OZ. POUCH .... **49¢**

MARSHMALLOWS 10-OZ. REG. 89¢ .... **69¢**

CHARCOAL BRIQUETS 10-LB. BAG **$4.99**

CHILI CON CARNE W/BEANS
REG. & HOT/40 OZ. CAN REG. $2.79 .... **$2.09**

LIQUID FLUID QT. TIN REG. 89¢ .... **69¢**

FRUIT PUNCH 48-OZ. JAR. REG. $1.79 .... **$1.49**

MUSHROOMS 4-OZ. CAN/PIECES & STEMS. REG. 65¢ .... **59¢**

CHEESE HORNS $1.79
MILD COLBY, RED WAX CHEDDAR

AMERICAN $1.89
CHEESE, 12-OZ. PKG. REG. $2.45

SOFT CHEESE 89¢
4½-OZ. PKG. REG. $1.09

SNACK CRACKERS

ASSORTED VARIETY
REG. $1.79

$1.39

"From now on," Jennifer said, "I'll do all my shopping at the Thrift Mart. We would save $3.99 on the items on this list."

"That isn't very much," Bill said. "But multiply $3.99 times 52 weeks. At that rate, we'd save $207.48 in a year."

"But wait!" Mrs. Rossi said. "We could save more than $3.99 this week. Four items on my list cost less at the Super Saver. We could buy these four items at the Super Saver Market. Then we could buy the other 11 items at the Thrift Mart."

	Super Saver	Thrift Mart
3 lbs. pork spareribs	$7.17	$9.25
1 lb. cherries	2.19	2.49
2 heads lettuce	1.39	1.52
charcoal briquets	4.89	4.99

Would you take the time to compare food prices if you could save this much (or more) every year?

10. How much would these four items cost at the Super Saver Market? _____

11. How much would the same four items cost at the Thrift Mart? _____

12. How much money is saved by buying these items at the Super Saver Market? _____

13. Suppose Mrs. Rossi buys these four items from the Super Saver. Then she buys the other 11 items from the Thrift Mart. How much will the 15 items cost all together? _____

"Now is a good time to buy frozen vegetables," said Mrs. Rossi. "In the summer, people like to eat fresh vegetables. There is less need for frozen food. So the price of frozen vegetables goes down."

"But there are no frozen vegetables in these newspaper ads," Jennifer said.

"Let's walk over to the shopping center," Mrs. Rossi said. "We'll compare prices on frozen foods."

While they walked, Mrs. Rossi talked about brand names. Each company has its own brand name. That's the name you see on the label. Some frozen-food makers are very well known. You hear their brand names on TV. But the big chain food stores have their own brand names. These labels are not as well known. But the food is often very good. And often it costs less than the well-known brand.

The Thrift Mart stores had their own label. Their brand was called "Pennywise." The Super Saver Markets called their brand "Superior." Bill, Jennifer, and Mrs. Rossi visited both stores. They compared prices on the 10-ounce boxes of frozen vegetables.

Here are the labels from three different brands of tomato sauce. How many different brands of tomato sauce are sold in your own food store? Which one costs the least?

Here are the prices they found at the Thrift Mart:

Vegetable	Pennywise	Well-known Brand
green beans	.55	.64
lima beans	.75	.69
broccoli	.59	.65
Brussels sprouts	1.09	1.49
corn	.55	.75
peas	.55	.75

1. a. Mrs. Rossi wants to buy one box of each frozen vegetable. How much would she pay for the well-known brand? _____

b. How much would she pay for the Pennywise brand? _____

c. How much could she save by buying Pennywise? _____

Jennifer made a list of the Pennywise prices for six different vegetables. Then Bill, Jennifer, and Mrs. Rossi went to the Super Saver Market. They compared prices of the Pennywise brand and the Superior brand.

Vegetable	Pennywise	Superior
green beans	.55	.57
lima beans	.75	.79
broccoli	.59	.64
Brussels sprouts	1.09	1.39
corn	.55	3 for 1.53
peas	.55	3 for 1.53

2. a. Suppose Bill bought *three boxes* of each vegetable. How much would he pay for the Pennywise brand? _____

b. How much would he pay for the Superior brand? _____

c. How much would he save by buying Pennywise vegetables? _____

Superior brand corn and peas are "specials" this week. At three for $1.53, they cost less than the Pennywise brand.

3. Suppose Bill buys all the Pennywise vegetables *except* corn and peas. Then he buys the Superior brand corn and peas. He buys three boxes of each vegetable on the list. How much will he spend all together? _____

4. You can save money by comparing prices of different brands. Another way to save money is to buy food in the large-size cans or boxes.

Pennywise coffee costs $3.99 a pound in the 1-pound can. The 2-pound can costs $5.59.

a. Suppose Jennifer buys two 1-pound cans of coffee each month. How much will she spend on coffee in one year? _____

b. Suppose Jennifer buys one 2-pound can of coffee every month. How much will she spend on coffee in one year? _____

c. How much can she save per year by buying coffee in 2-pound cans? _____

READING FOOD LABELS

What is in the canned orange juice you drink for breakfast? Is it made from oranges? Or is it made of water, sugar, and flavoring? Find out by reading the label.

What is in your breakfast cereal? Cereals are made of grains, like wheat, oats, and corn. But some cereal boxes contain more sugar than cereal. On these boxes, sugar is named first on the label.

Food labels include a "Nutrition Facts" panel which gives information about important nutrients. **Nutrients** are the raw materials that build strong bodies. You get nutrients from milk, meat, eggs, fruit, vegetables, bread, and cereal. But many families do not get enough nutrients in their food.

The U.S. Department of Agriculture has learned which nutrients people need and how much a person needs of each nutrient. These key nutrients are listed on labels: total fat and saturated fat, cholesterol, sodium, total carbohydrates including fiber and sugars, protein, vitamins A and C, calcium, and iron.

The amount of nutrients in a food can be given either in grams or as a percentage of the **Daily Value. % Daily Value** shows how a serving of food fits into all the food you eat in one day if you eat 2,000 calories each day.

Each day you should eat 100% of the Daily Value for each nutrient. Nutrients such as fat and sodium should not go over

100% percent. But you should eat at least 100% of nutrients such as fiber, calcium, and vitamins A and C.

Protein is the basic material in every cell in your body. Calcium and iron are minerals.

After each nutrient on the label you will find a number. The number is a percentage. Suppose the label says "Calcium . . . 6." Then you will know that one serving of this food contains 6% of the calcium that you need in one day.

Here are the labels from two 8-ounce cans of tomato sauce. Compare Label A and Label B. Then answer each question by writing A or B in the blank.

_____ 1. Which can contains the most protein?

_____ 2. Which can contains the most vitamin A?

_____ 3. Which can contains the most vitamin C?

_____ 4. Which can contains the most sodium?

_____ 5. Which can contains the most carbohydrates?

_____ 6. Which can contains the most sugars?

_____ 7. Which can contains the most calcium?

A

Nutrition Facts
Serving Size 8 oz
Servings Per Container 1

Calories 80
Fat Calories 0

	% Daily Value*
Total Fat 0g	0%
Saturated Fat 0g	0%
Cholesterol 0mg	0%
Sodium 550mg	23%
Total Carbohydrates 19g	6%
Dietary Fiber 3g	11%
Sugars 13g	
Protein 2g	

Vitamin A 50%	Vitamin C 30%
Calcium 2%	Iron 10%

*Percent Daily Values (DV) are based on a 2,000 calorie diet.

INGREDIENTS: TOMATO PUREE (WATER, TOMATO PASTE), SALT, ONIONS, GARLIC POWDER, CORN SYRUP, SPICES, NATURAL FLAVOR.

B

Nutrition Facts
Serving Size 8 oz
Servings Per Container 1

Calories 100
Fat Calories 10

	% Daily Value*
Total Fat 1g	2%
Saturated Fat 0.5g	3%
Cholesterol 0mg	0%
Sodium 400mg	17%
Total Carbohydrates 17g	5%
Dietary Fiber 2g	8%
Sugars 10g	
Protein 4g	

Vitamin A 60%	Vitamin C 60%
Calcium 4%	Iron 10%

*Percent Daily Values (DV) are based on a 2,000 calorie diet.

INGREDIENTS: TOMATO PUREE (TOMATO PASTE AND WATER), DICED TOMATOES, CORN OIL, ONIONS, CORN SYRUP, SALT, SPICES, NATURAL FLAVOR.

SHOPPING FOR NUTRITION— NOT JUST CALORIES!

"Hi, Jennifer! Come in and have a cup of coffee!" Jennifer saw Ann coming up the hall with two big bags of groceries. Ann lived at Holly House in apartment #8.

Jennifer carried one of the grocery bags to Ann's kitchen. Then she drank coffee while Ann unpacked the bags.

"My grocery bills are too high," Ann said. "So I've been watching the ads to see what's on sale. All these things were on sale at the Thrift Mart—even the nail polish. I used a **coupon** from the Sunday paper—$1 off when I bought two bottles."

Ann had bought soft drinks, candy, cookies, potato chips, nail polish, and magazines.

"But where is the food?" Jennifer asked. "You bought snacks, drinks, and things to read and wear. You can't live on stuff like that! Where are the meat and vegetables?"

Ann looked at the things she had bought. Then she said, "You're right! No wonder my grocery bills are so high! And no wonder I'm putting on weight! There are lots of **calories** in this food. But there isn't much nutrition in it."

Snack foods like potato chips are high in fats (such as cooking oils). Candy, cookies, and many soft drinks are high in sugars. People need both fats and sugars in their **diets.** But you get enough fats and sugars in your meals. These snack foods and drinks can make you fat—but they can't make you healthy.

It's fine to buy some items such as magazines or shampoo at the grocery store. But be careful. These things often cost more at a grocery store than at a discount drugstore. Many coupons are good only if you buy two or more of an item. You may end up buying more than you need. And

Words to Know	When Shopping for Food

coupon: a ticket that lets you buy a product for less than the price stamped on the can or package. Coupons are found in newspapers, magazines, and on labels and food packages.

calories: the amount of energy you get from the food you eat. Most fruits and vegetables are low in calories. Fats, starches, and sugars are high in calories. You gain weight when your food gives you more calories than you need.

diet: all the foods a person eats.

grocery stores often place snacks or non-food items right near the checkstands. It's easy to buy something you weren't planning to buy. You can save money by making a list ahead of time and then buying only what's on the list.

How much do snack foods, drinks, and extra items add to a family's supermarket bill? Find out by using Ann's "groceries" as an example. Ann bought these items:

1 6-pack of soft drinks	$1.59
3 bags of candy	2.69
1 bag of cookies	1.59
1 bag of potato chips	1.29
2 bottles of nail polish	5.00
2 magazines	4.40

1. How much did she spend for all these items? _____

2. Suppose Ann spends the same amount every two weeks on snacks, drinks, and extra items. How much will she spend on these items in a year? (Remember, there are 52 weeks in a year.) _____

3. The regular price of cola was $2.25 for a six-pack. Suppose a person drinks six colas a week. How much does this person spend on cola in a year? _____

4. One magazine costs $1.95. Another costs $2.50. Suppose a person buys each magazine every two weeks for a year. How much will the magazine bill add up to in a year? _____

5. Ann buys two pairs of nylons a month. The nylons cost $3.75 at the grocery store and $2.29 at the discount drugstore. If she buys nylons at the drugstore for a year, how much will she save? _____

NAIL POLISH
WHEN YOU BUY 2 — EA. **$2.50**

MAGAZINES
FROM **$1.95**

COLA
SOFT DRINKS
6 PAK 12 OZ. CANS **$1.59**

JELLY CANDIES
ASSORTED 10 OZ. BAGS
3 FOR **$2.69**

POTATO CHIPS
8 OZ. SIZE REGULAR $1.49
SAVE 20¢ **$1.29**

COOKIES
18 OZ. BAG **$1.59**

Jennifer wanted to make a rice pudding. She looked for rice in her cupboard. There was a big box of brown rice, but no white rice. Jennifer asked Bill if he would please go to the store. She asked him to buy "a small box of white rice."

Bill went to the food store and found three kinds of white rice:

- long-grain rice
- converted rice
- quick (or instant) rice

Bill checked the prices on the small boxes. At first he thought the boxes were all the same size. Then he picked up two different boxes. One box felt heavy and the other box felt light. Bill read the labels. The heavy box held 16 ounces. The light box held only 7 ounces.

Bill needed to find the cost of one ounce of each kind of rice. Then he could compare prices.

First Bill looked at the quick rice. It cost $1.15 for 7 ounces. To find the cost per ounce, Bill divided the price by the number of ounces.

$$\begin{array}{r} .16 \\ 7\overline{)1.15} \\ -7 \\ \hline 45 \\ -42 \\ \hline 3 \end{array}$$

One ounce of quick rice costs about 16 cents.

1. What is the cost of one ounce of converted rice at 16 ounces for $1.35? _____

2. What is the cost of one ounce of long-grain rice at 14 ounces for $.69? _____

Why do quick rice and converted rice cost more? Converted rice is white rice that has been treated to add more nutrition. Quick rice is rice that has already been cooked. When you buy this type of food, you have to pay for any extra work that other people do for you!

Suppose quick rice and converted rice are the same price per ounce in your store. By reading the labels, you find that:

- $\frac{2}{3}$ cup of quick rice makes two servings.
- 1 cup of converted rice makes six servings.

3. Which kind costs less per serving? _____

When you compare prices in newspaper ads, be sure to check the *sizes*. Look at these two ads for lemonade.

4. Super Saver is selling the 6-ounce size for 38 cents a can. What is the price per ounce? _____

5. Thrift Mart is selling two 12-ounce cans for $1.68. What is the price per ounce? _____

6. Which lemonade is the best buy—two 6-ounce cans or one 12-ounce can? _____

In many food stores you can compare prices the easy way. Look for small signs like these on the shelves. These signs show that lime juice costs much less if you buy it in the big bottle. In 7-ounce bottles, lime juice costs $2.70 a pint. But in the 25-ounce bottles, it costs only $1.46 a pint.

These signs show the price of stuffed olives. Suppose you want some olives for a picnic. Can you read the signs?

7. How much is the cost *per ounce* of olives in a 7-ounce jar? _____

8. How much is the cost *per ounce* of olives in an 8.5-ounce jar? _____

9. How much is the cost *per ounce* of olives in a 10-ounce jar? _____

10. Which jar of olives is the best buy? _____

Before Easter, you will find hams in most food store ads. You may see the word HAM in big type beside a picture. And you may also see that the price is low, compared to prices in other stores. Such items are "specials." The ham is sold at a low price just to bring people to the store. The managers hope you will spend *all* of your food dollars in their store! But if you have compared prices on other items too, you will probably buy from more than one place.

Watch for "specials" and buy them to save money.

Consumer Tip

When you buy food, you have to pay for any extra work that other people do for you. Food that is cooked (like quick rice) costs more than food that is raw. You have to pay for the work that goes into the cooking. Usually a canned ham costs more than a ham that is not canned. You have to pay for the work that goes into the canning.

EXERCISE 32

1. If a 5-pound ham costs $8.89, what is the price per pound? _____

2. If a 5-pound ham costs $9.99, what is the price per pound? _____

This ad shows how *work* adds to the cost of food.

3. If an 8-pound ham costs $14.32, what is the price per pound? _____

4. If this same ham is sliced, you pay $15.32 for 8 pounds. Now what is the price per pound? _____

CANNED HAMS

HAM

8 LB.

(SLICED $15.32) **$14.32**

1. Sue Takata's parents are retired. Mr. Takata gets a check every month from a retirement fund. Both Mr. and Mrs. Takata get social security checks. When prices go up, workers may get pay raises to meet the cost of living. People on Social Security get a small increase once a year. The amount is set (or "fixed") by the U.S. government, so we say they are on a "fixed" income.

   Many retired people do not get good nutrition because they have so little money to spend on food. And sometimes they are in very poor health. If so, they cannot go out to do their own food shopping. How does your city or town help retired people?

2. Mr. Takata has been gaining too much weight. And he has not been eating the right foods. His doctor gave him a list of low-calorie foods high in nutrition. Plan three low-calorie lunches for Mr. Takata using foods from this list.

apples	lamb (lean)
beans	lettuce
(green or wax)	low-calorie
beets	salad dressing
bread	orange juice
carrots	(unsweetened)
celery	peaches
chicken (no skin)	pears
crab	pickles
cucumbers	skim milk
cottage cheese	spinach
eggs	tomatoes
grapefruit	veal (lean)

TAKE THIS COUPON TO YOUR STORE 25¢

Clip coupons from your newspaper. Use them when you go shopping.

25¢

TAKE THIS COUPON TO YOUR STORE 25¢

Using coupons can be a good way to save money on food.

25¢

Consumer Tip

Be careful when using coupons! Often they are for high-priced foods that have very little nutrition. Sometimes they are for foods you wouldn't buy anyway or for things you don't need. And usually they are for brand-name items that can cost more than less well-known brands—even with the coupon!

TEST YOURSELF

Use prices in the ads to answer these questions.

Suppose you want to buy five pounds of ground beef and two pounds of trout.

1. How much will these two items cost at the Super Saver? _____

2. How much will these two items cost at the Thrift Mart? _____

Suppose you buy a 12-ounce package of lunch meat at the Super Saver.

3. How much is the price per ounce? _____

4. How much is the price per pound? (There are 16 ounces in a pound.) _____

Suppose you are shopping at the Thrift Mart. You want to serve a meal to six people.

5. You know that one pound of boneless round steak makes three servings. How much will it cost to serve round steak to six people? _____

6. You know that one pound of pork loin roast makes only two servings. How much will it cost to serve pork loin roast to six people? _____

7. You can make three hamburgers from a pound of ground beef. How much will it cost to serve hamburgers to six people? _____

SUPER SAVER MARKET

| LUNCH MEAT ASSORTED VARIETIES IN 12 OZ. PKGS! EACH **$2.19** | BEEF ROAST RUMP OR SIRLOIN TIP ROASTS LB. **$1.77** |

BEEF CUBE STEAKS .... LB. $1.99
HEEL OF ROUND ROAST ...... LB. $1.48
BONELESS RND. STEAK ...... LB. $1.98
BONELESS HAM .... LB. $2.99
DOVER SOLE............... LB. $2.99

| IDAHO TROUT FRESH! TENDER PAN SIZE LB. **$4.99** | GROUND BEEF FRESH REGULAR IN 5 LB. CHUBS! LB. **99¢** |

THRIFT MART

GROUND BEEF
DOES NOT EXCEED 30% FAT.
ANY SIZE PKG.
LB. **$1.19**

BEEF ROUND STEAK
BONELESS, FULL CUT
LB. **$2.99**

BEEF RIB ROAST
(SMALL END LB. $2.29) LARGE END .... LB. $1.89
PORK LOIN ROAST
3½–4 LBS., FINEST EASTERN................... LB. $2.88
TURKEY HAM
FULLY COOKED, NATURAL HICKORY SMOKED .... LB. $1.88
FRESH TROUT FILLETS
GRADE A .... LB. $3.99

ANSWERS:
6. $8.64 7. $2.38
1. $14.93 2. $13.93 3. 18¢ 4. $2.88 5. $5.98

What did you eat yesterday for breakfast, lunch, dinner, and snacks? Write each food down on a piece of paper.

For good nutrition, you need foods from each of the groups shown in the Food Guide Pyramid below. Read the number of servings you need from each group every day. Then read the list of what counts as a serving in each group. Put a (✔) in the box on the right for each serving that you ate yesterday. (If you ate two servings of the same food, put two checks in that box.) Did your diet match the recommendations of the food pyramid? For a healthful diet, fats, oils, and sweets should be used sparingly.

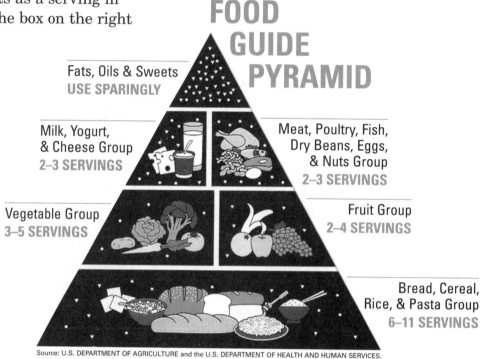

FOOD GUIDE PYRAMID

Fats, Oils & Sweets
USE SPARINGLY

Milk, Yogurt, & Cheese Group
2–3 SERVINGS

Meat, Poultry, Fish, Dry Beans, Eggs, & Nuts Group
2–3 SERVINGS

Vegetable Group
3–5 SERVINGS

Fruit Group
2–4 SERVINGS

Bread, Cereal, Rice, & Pasta Group
6–11 SERVINGS

Source: U.S. DEPARTMENT OF AGRICULTURE and the U.S. DEPARTMENT OF HEALTH AND HUMAN SERVICES.

WHAT COUNTS AS A SERVING?

Check for each serving you ate yesterday

Bread, Cereal, Rice, Pasta Group (6-11 servings)									
1 slice of bread	1 ounce of ready-to-eat cereal	$\frac{1}{2}$ cup of cooked rice, cereal, or pasta							
Vegetable Group (3-5 servings)									
1 cup of raw leafy vegetables	$\frac{1}{2}$ cup of other vegetables, cooked or chopped raw	$\frac{3}{4}$ cup of vegetable juice							
Fruit Group (2-4 servings)									
1 medium apple, banana, orange	$\frac{1}{2}$ cup of chopped, cooked, or canned fruit	$\frac{3}{4}$ cup of fruit juice							
Milk, Yogurt, and Cheese Group (2-3 servings)									
1 cup of milk or yogurt	$1\frac{1}{2}$ ounces of natural cheese	2 ounces of process cheese							
Meat, Poultry, Fish, Dry Beans, Eggs, and Nuts Group (2-3 servings)									
2–3 ounces of cooked lean meat, poultry, or fish	$\frac{1}{2}$ cup of cooked dry beans, 1 egg, or 2 tablespoons of peanut butter count as 1 ounce of lean meat								

Buying a Car

NAME _____

Preview: What a Car Costs

Suppose you have saved $1,000 and you want to buy a car. Should you take "the #1 deal" in this ad? Read the ad carefully before you decide "yes" or "no." Be sure you know how much the car will cost you.

Use the ad to answer these questions:

1. How much is the cash price of the car? _____

2. How much is the down payment, plus tax, title, and registration fee? _____

3. How much is the monthly payment? _____

4. For how many years will you make these monthly payments? _____

5. What rate of interest (APR) will you pay? _____

6. How much will the car cost you all together? _____

7. How much interest will you pay in 60 months? _____

BEAT THE CLOCK SPECIAL

$99 DOWN

$169.97 per month for 60 months. Cash price $7599, plus $533.68 tax, title, and registration. 12.75% Annual Percentage Rate. Total payments $10,198.20

The #1 Deal $169.97 MO.

ANSWERS:

1. $7,599 2. $632.68 3. $169.97 4. five 5. 12.75% 6. $10,830.88 7. $2,599.20

Buying a Car

On Labor Day, Bill and Jennifer went to a picnic with Ed and Anne Thomas and their children. Bill asked questions about the Thomases' new car. The big question was, "How do you decide which car to buy?"

"Easy," said Ed. "We read the magazine *Consumer Reports*. It is printed by a group called Consumers Union. They test new cars and other products. Then they tell you which ones they think are the best."

"Do you know anything about **leasing** a new car?" asked Bill.

"We almost leased a car," said Anne. "We liked the idea of getting a new car without having to pay money up front. A new car does not have the problems that a used car can have."

"Why didn't you lease a new car?" Jennifer asked.

"The payments were too high for us," Anne answered. "So we decided to look for a secondhand car."

"We've been thinking about buying a secondhand car," Bill said. "But used cars are even harder to pick out than new cars. And we don't know very much about cars."

"Neither do I," Ed answered. "But my brother Al is a **mechanic.** If you find a used car that you like, I'll ask him to check it out for you."

At the picnic, Ed and Anne explained how they picked out their car. They had started with three questions:

1. "How big a car do we need?"

    Ed and Anne wanted a small car because a little car uses less gas. Year in and year out, it would cost less to run.

| Words to Know | When Buying a Car |

leasing: making monthly payments for the use of a new car for a 2 to 3 year period; after which the car must be returned to the dealer or the remaining purchase price paid.

mechanic: a person who repairs car engines.

subcompact: the smallest car that seats four people.

compact: a middle-size car.

dealer: a person who sells cars.

options: extras you can buy on a car that add to the price of the car.

The smallest cars that seat four people are called **subcompacts.** But a subcompact does not have much room in the back seat. Since the Thomases had children, they wanted more space.

Middle-size cars are called **compacts.** These cars are big enough for five or six people but still small enough to save gas. Anne and Ed chose a four-door compact. A four-door car is easy to get into and out of.

2. "Which four-door compact should we choose?"

    That year, Consumers Union picked four compacts that were very good. Ed and Anne looked at all four of them. They talked to people who owned them. They asked questions about the **dealers** who sold the cars. They wanted to buy from a dealer who would give them good service.

3. "Which **options** do we want on our car?"

Options are "extras," like a sunroof or power steering. Every option you choose adds to the price of the car. Suppose the car costs $10,000. Power steering adds about $250 to that price. A sunroof adds about $550. Every "extra" that you put on a car pushes the price up higher.

The Thomases had to shop around to find the car they wanted. They often had to say "no" to dealers who wanted to sell them fancy cars.

One dealer told them: "If you order a car from Detroit, you may have to wait three months to get it. Why don't you buy this green car? You can have it right away."

Anne and Ed looked at the green car in the dealer's lot. They read the sticker on the car window. They saw that the options on the green car added up to $4,268.

Ed and Anne shopped around until they found the same car without so many options.

The Thomases had not planned to buy an air-conditioned car. Air conditioning adds about $700–$800 to the price of a car. Also, the air conditioner uses extra gas. You might get 30 miles per gallon on cool days. But on hot days when the air conditioning is turned on, you might get only 26 miles per gallon.

In the end, the Thomases did buy the air-conditioned car. Where they live, there are summer days when the temperature goes above 100 degrees!

Ed and Anne picked out a car that cost $10,065. Then they decided on the first five options listed at the right.

1. How much did these options add to the cost of the car? _____

2. Before the options were added, the price of the car was $10,065. How much did the car cost with the options added on? _____

3. The Thomases had to pay 7% sales tax. How much did they pay in sales tax? _____

4. The Thomases had to pay two more charges: $40 for new license plates and $50 for the title (a paper showing that they own the car).

Options	Function	Cost
Automatic transmission	Makes driving easy. Car is easy to sell later on.	$815
Luggage rack & rear window wiper/washer	Rack makes it easier to transport oversized cargo. Wiper improves visibility.	$240
Anti-lock braking system	Important safety feature	$570
AM/FM stereo	Makes driving more fun.	$300
Air conditioning	Keeps the car cool on hot days. Uses extra gas.	$785
Sun roof	Helps to keep the car cool. Costs less than air conditioning.	$525

Car _____

Options _____

Tax _____

Plates _____

Title _____

TOTAL _____

When Ed saw the price, he said, "I'll give you $13,300 for the car." The dealer said OK. So the Thomases had a new car!

Jennifer and Bill began to look at new cars. They were not ready to buy. But it was fun to test-drive the new subcompacts! And they wanted to learn as much as they could about buying cars.

They were also learning about **finance charges.** You have to pay finance charges when you borrow money to buy a car. But if you make a big down payment, the **loan** will cost less. Then you can save more money by paying off the loan in a very short time. So Jennifer and Bill wanted to save up a big down payment.

But at each car lot, they met salespeople who wanted to "make a deal." One dealer said, "You don't need a big down payment. Just pay $299 down. After that, you pay $90 a month."

Words to Know	About Finance Charges

finance charge: a fee that is charged for using credit.

loan: money that is borrowed.

Annual Percentage Rate (APR): the percent-per-year rate that is charged for using credit. A U.S. law says that the person who gives credit must tell you what the rate is.

Bill and Jennifer began to ask about finance charges. Because of the Truth-in-Lending law, the dealer must tell the buyer the amount of finance charges for each deal. The rate is called the **Annual Percentage Rate (APR).** It is different on each "deal."

Here are some of the "deals" that Jennifer and Bill found while shopping for a car.

In late summer, dealers try to sell cars as fast as they can. They want to make room for the new cars that will soon come out. Some dealers try to outsell each other by cutting prices. Here are four "deals" for the same car, with different options. Use the prices in each ad to find the total cost of the car and the loan. Do not use the APR. It has already been figured in the monthly terms and the down payment.

Deal A

$152.77 PER MONTH

Down payment: $2,500. Tax and registration: $593.55, APR 11.10%.
$152.77 per month for 60 months.

1. How much is the total cost? _____

_____ monthly payment   _____ total of payments

× _____ number of payments   _____ down payment

_____ total of payments   + _____ tax and registration

_____ total cost of the car

2. The cash price of this car is $9,595 plus tax and registration. How much would the car cost if the buyer paid cash? _____

3. How much is the cost of the loan (the interest)? _____

Deal B

$147.98 PER MONTH

Down payment: $2,500. APR 11.64%. Tax and registration: $566.55, $147.98 per month for 60 months.

4. How much is the total cost of the car? _____

5. The cash price of this car is $9,295 plus tax and registration. How much would the car cost if the buyer paid cash? _____

6. How much is the cost of the loan? _____

Deal C

$156.97 PER MONTH

Down payment: $2,100. APR 12.15%. Tax and registration: $561.06, $156.97 per month for 60 months.

7. How much is the total cost of the car? _____

8. The cash price of this car is $9,234 plus tax and registration. How much would the car cost if the buyer paid cash? _____

9. How much is the cost of the loan? _____

Deal D

$254.00 PER MONTH

Down payment: $0. APR 10.62%. Tax and registration: $628.92, $254 per month for 48 months.

10. How much is the total cost? _____

11. The cash price of the car is $9,988 plus tax and registration. How much would the car cost if the buyer paid cash? _____

12. How much is the cost of the loan? _____

Put an X beside the correct answer.

13. Which deal has the lowest APR?

_____ Deal A _____ Deal C

_____ Deal B _____ Deal D

14. Which deal has the lowest down payment?

_____ Deal A _____ Deal C

_____ Deal B _____ Deal D

15. In which deal must the loan be paid off in four years?

_____ Deal A _____ Deal C

_____ Deal B _____ Deal D

16. Which of these items changes the cost of the loan?

_____ **a.** the APR

_____ **b.** the size of the down payment

_____ **c.** a long or short time to pay off the loan

_____ **d.** all of the above

December is a good time to buy a car. Many people are shopping for the holidays, and cars are not selling well. Some dealers cut prices and run big ads in the paper.

By this December, Bill had saved $3,800 in his credit union account. And he wanted a car very badly. Bill showed Jennifer an ad: "Subcompacts as low as $7,425!"

The ad was for a used Toyota. Bill explained why he liked that car: "Consumers Union tested all the small cars for that year. This car got a very high score on their test."

On Saturday morning, Jennifer and Bill took the bus to San Juan Toyota and asked to see the car in the ad. "That car has been sold," the saleswoman said. "But I have another one almost like it right here." Jennifer and Bill liked the car she showed them. But the price was $8,758. They thanked the saleswoman and took the bus back home.

Now they had another idea: they would buy a car from a private owner. And before they bought it, they would ask Al Thomas—Ed's brother—to check it over. In the used-car ads, they found two 2-year-old Toyotas for less than $8,000. They wanted to look at both cars.

"This time we won't have to take the bus," Bill said. "I'll ask the owners to drive their cars over to our place."

Both Toyotas turned out to be nice clean cars. The green one had 20,000 miles on it, and the owner wanted $7,950. The yellow one had gone only 16,000 miles and looked like new. The owner was asking for $7,500. Bill and Jennifer liked the yellow car best.

Both owners took their cars to the place where Al Thomas worked. Al checked the yellow one first. "Don't buy the yellow car,"

| Words to Know | When Buying a Used Car |

blue book: the National Automobile Dealers Association (NADA) Official Used Car Guide. It gives the wholesale ("low blue book") price and the retail ("high blue book") price for used cars.

wholesale: the price a dealer pays.

retail: the price a dealer charges.

he said. "That car has been in a very bad accident. The frame is bent out of shape."

Then Al checked the green car. "The green one is a good used car," Al said. "Make an offer on it. But first, let's check the **blue book** and find out how much it's worth. Then we will know the **wholesale** price and the **retail** price."

$8,800 retail
$6,776 wholesale

1. How much would a dealer make on a used Ford truck at these prices? _____

2. You can save money in a private sale because you do not have to pay for the dealer's services. Here's one way to find a fair price for a good used car in a private sale. Add the wholesale and retail prices together, then divide by two to find the average. How much is the average of the two prices for the used Ford truck? _____

3. Clip car and truck ads from your newspaper. Circle these words when you find them:

- Purchase
- Lease

Suppose an ad says, "$199 a month for 36 months." If you *purchase* this car, you will own it after five years. You are buying the car by making the 36 payments. But if you *lease* the car, you will be paying just to use it. You will not own the car after the three years.

In most cases, you can purchase a car after you lease it for a period of time. Look for the word *residual* in car-leasing ads. For example,

"Option to purchase at end of lease for residual of $1,770."

In this deal, you must first make monthly payments for a certain length of time. Then you must pay another $1,770 if you want to keep the car.

Consumer Tip

If you are buying a used car, you can make an offer that is lower than the average. If you are selling a car, you can ask for more than the average. The selling price is any amount that the buyer and seller can agree on.

Jennifer and Bill paid Al $60 for checking the two used cars. They wanted to pay for his time. And they knew he had saved them far more than $60.

"Without Al's help," Bill said, "we might have bought that yellow car. Then we'd really be in trouble!"

Bill and Jennifer needed to borrow $4,200. They had planned to borrow the money from the credit union. But the credit union's APR had gone up to 7%.

Jennifer thought they could do better than that. She said, "On Monday I'll call some banks and ask about their interest rates." She had to act fast. Nancy Martin, the owner of the car, wanted her money right away.

Sunset Bank ran an ad in the Sunday paper. They would give low-cost loans on new cars. The annual percentage rate would be 9.75%.

"I've never heard of Sunset Bank," said Jennifer. "It must be a very small bank."

Small banks often lend money at lower interest rates than larger banks. Jennifer learned that when she called the banks on Monday. She called Central Bank and National Savings and Loan. She also called some other places, but Sunset Bank had the lowest APR.

The 9.75% rate was for new cars only. Sunset bank charged 11.50% for used-car loans. Sunset Bank would lend up to 100% of the low blue book price. They could pay off the loan in five years.

"We want to borrow $4,200," Jennifer said. "And we want to pay it back in four years."

The bank asked for credit references. Bill and Jennifer gave three references: Central Bank, the credit union, and the department store where they had their charge account.

On Friday Nancy Martin met Jennifer and Bill at the bank. Sunset Bank had to make sure that the car was in good shape and that Nancy was the real owner. Jennifer and Bill took time to read the contract they had to sign. They asked questions until they knew all the terms of the loan.

At last, Nancy Martin went home on the bus. Bill and Jennifer drove home in a little green car!

1. Suppose you want to borrow $3,000 to buy a car. You want to pay back the loan in three years. The dealer will lend you the money at 11.10%. A credit union will lend you the money at 8%.

How much will you save by borrowing from the credit union? _____

$3,000 loan/36 months to pay		
Annual Percentage Rate	Monthly Payment	Total Finance Charges
Credit Union 8.00%	$93.63	$370.68
Dealer 11.10%	$97.61	$513.96

2. Sue Takata borrowed $3,000 from Sunset Bank. She paid off the loan in 24 payments of $135.94 each. How much was her total finance charge? _____

NEED A NEW CAR, VAN, OR PICKUP?

8.5%
Annual Percentage Rate

LOW COST LOANS ON NEW CARS, VANS & PICKUPS

Then you also need our 8.5% Annual Percentage Rate financing to help keep your costs down. It could mean the difference in your ability to get the vehicle you want . . . and this rate is the full charge for your loan . . . no other costs or fees. Come in! We'll tell you just how much your monthly payments will be on any given loan.

SUNSET BANK • 7630 CARLTON STREET

THINGS TO FIND OUT WHEN BUYING A CAR

1. When you buy a new car, you should get a *warranty* from the dealer. A warranty is a paper that says the dealer will fix your car if there is something wrong with it. Most new-car warranties cover the car for 12 months or 12,000 miles. Sometimes you can get a warranty on a used car. Find some warranties to read and discuss in class.

2. Each state has laws about selling, owning, and driving cars. Before you drive a car, you should learn about these laws.

3. Do you have to pay a state tax when you buy a car? In this chapter, there is a 7% sales tax in each example. Find out how much tax you would pay on each of these cars in your own state.

4. Under a state law, Jennifer and Bill had to buy auto insurance before they could drive their car. Their insurance plan would pay *others* for any damages caused by their car. Everyone who drives a car needs auto insurance, but your state may call for a different kind. Find out what kind of insurance you need and how much it costs.

Consumer Tip

If you take driver's training classes, it may save you money on car insurance. And it may make you a safer driver! Find out about classes in your area.

TEST YOURSELF

Answer these questions. You'll find the answers in the ads.

Deal A

PURCHASE

Nothing Down!
$299 per mo.

Cash price of $12,726.61. 60-month financing with credit approval. Payment of title and registration fees of $1,145.39 is separate. Deferred price— $19,085.39. Annual Percentage Rate—10.6%.

Deal B

BRAND NEW FULL PURCHASE
ONLY **$131.02** per mo.

Only $131.02 per month for 60 months with credit OK. Just $1,500 down, includes title and registration. Deferred payment price—$9,361.20. Annual Percentage Rate—12.50%. Purchase price—$6,695, plus $602.55 tax and license. Brand new 3-door.

1. How much is the Annual Percentage Rate in Deal A? _____

2. How much are title and registration for this car? _____

3. How much is the cash price for this car? _____

4. How much is the deferred price—the total cost of the car, the title and registration, and the loan? _____

5. How much is the Annual Percentage Rate in Deal B? _____

6. How much is the down payment for this car? _____

7. How much is the cash price for this car? _____

8. How much is the total cost of the car, the title and registration, and the loan? _____

ANSWERS:

8. $9,361.20
4. $19,085.39 5. 12.5% 6. $1,500 7. $7,297.55
1. 10.6% 2. $1,145.39 3. $12,726.61

Beside each sentence, write T for true or F for false.

_____ **1.** A compact car is smaller than a subcompact.

_____ **2.** Air conditioning uses extra gas.

_____ **3.** A finance charge is a fee for options.

_____ **4.** APR means Automobile Parts and Repair.

_____ **5.** A car costs less if you pay cash for it than if you make payments on it.

_____ **6.** The "low blue book" price is the wholesale price of a used car.

_____ **7.** The "high blue book" price is the retail price of a used car.

_____ **8.** When you buy a used car from a dealer, you pay the low blue book price.

_____ **9.** You can use the APR to compare finance charges.

_____ **10.** Big banks always charge less than small banks for new-car loans.

_____ **11.** All the options that you add to a new car cost extra.

_____ **12.** A car dealer must tell the buyer the amount of finance charges.

_____ **13.** Big cars use more gas than most small cars use.

_____ **14.** On new-car deals, the buyer does not pay for the title and registration.

_____ **15.** The selling price of a car is any amount that the buyer and the seller can agree on.

ANSWERS:

11. T   12. T   13. T   14. F   15. T

1. F   2. T   3. F   4. F   5. T   6. T   7. T   8. F   9. T   10. F